# The DAC Guidelines
## Poverty Reduction

OECD

ORGANISATION FOR ECONOMIC CO-OPERATION AND DEVELOPMENT

# ORGANISATION FOR ECONOMIC CO-OPERATION AND DEVELOPMENT

Pursuant to Article 1 of the Convention signed in Paris on 14th December 1960, and which came into force on 30th September 1961, the Organisation for Economic Co-operation and Development (OECD) shall promote policies designed:

- to achieve the highest sustainable economic growth and employment and a rising standard of living in Member countries, while maintaining financial stability, and thus to contribute to the development of the world economy;

- to contribute to sound economic expansion in Member as well as non-member countries in the process of economic development; and

- to contribute to the expansion of world trade on a multilateral, non-discriminatory basis in accordance with international obligations.

The original Member countries of the OECD are Austria, Belgium, Canada, Denmark, France, Germany, Greece, Iceland, Ireland, Italy, Luxembourg, the Netherlands, Norway, Portugal, Spain, Sweden, Switzerland, Turkey, the United Kingdom and the United States. The following countries became Members subsequently through accession at the dates indicated hereafter: Japan (28th April 1964), Finland (28th January 1969), Australia (7th June 1971), New Zealand (29th May 1973), Mexico (18th May 1994), the Czech Republic (21st December 1995), Hungary (7th May 1996), Poland (22nd November 1996), Korea (12th December 1996) and the Slovak Republic (14th December 2000). The Commission of the European Communities takes part in the work of the OECD (Article 13 of the OECD Convention).

*In order to achieve its aims the OECD has set up a number of specialised committees. One of these is the Development Assistance Committee, whose Members have agreed to secure an expansion of aggregate volume of resources made available to developing countries and to improve their effectiveness. To this end, Members periodically review together both the amount and the nature of their contributions to aid programmes, bilateral and multilateral, and consult each other on all other relevant aspects of their development assistance policies.*

*The Members of the Development Assistance Committee are Australia, Austria, Belgium, Canada, Denmark, Finland, France, Germany, Greece, Ireland, Italy, Japan, Luxembourg, the Netherlands, New Zealand, Norway, Portugal, Spain, Sweden, Switzerland, the United Kingdom, the United States and the Commission of the European Communities.*

*Publié en français sous le titre :*

Les lignes directrices du CAD
LA RÉDUCTION DE LA PAUVRETÉ

# Table of Contents

## TABLE

## FIGURES

## BOXES

# Acronyms and Abbreviations

| | |
|---|---|
| **AIDS** | Acquired Immune Deficiency Syndrome |
| **BMZ** | German Federal Ministry for Economic Co-operation and Development |
| **CCA** | Common Country Assessment |
| **CDF** | Comprehensive Development Framework |
| **CG** | Consultative Group |
| **CIDA** | Canadian International Development Agency |
| **CS** | Country Strategies |
| **CSO** | Civil Society Organisation |
| **DAC** | Development Assistance Committee |
| **DFID** | Department for International Development |
| **DHS** | Demographic and Health Survey |
| **EC** | European Commission (manages the European Community Aid Programme) |
| **ECG** | OECD Export Credit Group |
| **EU** | European Union |
| **FDI** | Foreign Direct Investment |
| **GATS** | General Agreement on Trade in Services |
| **GDI** | Gender-related Development Index |
| **GDP** | Gross Domestic Product |
| **GEM** | Gender Empowerment Measure |
| **GMOs** | Genetically Modified Organisms |
| **GSP** | Generalised System of Preferences |
| **GTZ** | German Agency for Technical Co-operation |
| **HDI** | Human Development Index |
| **HIPCs** | Heavily Indebted Poor Countries |
| **HIV** | Human Immune Deficiency Virus |
| **HPI-1** | Human Poverty Index (Developing Countries) |
| **HPI-2** | Human Poverty Index (OECD and Transition Countries) |
| **HDR** | Human Development Report from UNDP |
| **ICT** | Information and Communications Technology |
| **IDEA** | Institute for Democracy and Electoral Assistance |
| **IDG** | International Development Goal |
| **IFAD** | International Fund for Agricultural Development |
| **ILO** | International Labour Organisation |
| **IMF** | International Monetary Fund |
| **IPR** | Intellectual Property Rights |
| **IRDP** | Integrated Rural Development Programme |
| **ITC** | International Trade Centre |
| **IWG** | Interdisciplinary Working Group |
| **LDCs** | Least Developed Countries |
| **MDGs** | Millennium Development Goals |
| **MTFF** | Medium-Term Fiscal Framework |
| **NGO** | Non-governmental Organisation |
| **NSSD** | National Strategy for Sustainable Development |
| **ODA** | Official Development Assistance |
| **OECD** | Organisation for Economic Co-operation and Development |

| | |
|---|---|
| **PPP** | Purchasing Power Parity |
| **PPA** | Participatory Poverty Assessment |
| **PRS** | Poverty Reduction Strategy |
| **PRSP** | Poverty Reduction Strategy Paper |
| **RT** | Round Table |
| **Sida** | Swedish International Development Co-operation Agency |
| **SPA** | Strategic Partnership with Africa |
| **SWAp** | Sector-Wide Approach |
| **TC** | Technical Co-operation |
| **TRIPS** | Trade Related Intellectual Property Rights |
| **UN** | United Nations |
| **UNAIDS** | Joint United Nations Programme on HIV/AIDS |
| **UNCED** | United Nations Conference on Environment and Development |
| **UNCTAD** | United Nations Conference on Trade and Development |
| **UNDAF** | United Nations Development Assistance Framework |
| **UNDP** | United Nations Development Programme |
| **UNESCO** | United Nations Educational, Scientific and Cultural Organisation |
| **UNIFEM** | United Nations Development Fund for Women |
| **UN-SGA** | United Nations Special General Assembly |
| **USAID** | United States Agency for International Development |
| **WB** | World Bank |
| **WDR** | World Development Report of the World Bank |
| **WHO** | World Health Organisation |
| **WTO** | World Trade Organisation |

# RISING TO THE GLOBAL CHALLENGE: PARTNERSHIP FOR REDUCING WORLD POVERTY

## Policy Statement by the DAC High Level Meeting upon endorsement of the DAC Guidelines on Poverty Reduction, Paris, 25-26 April 2001

Developing countries have achieved remarkable, although uneven, improvements in living standards over the past 30 years, and development co-operation has played a strong supportive role. But poverty reduction, in the context of sustainable development, remains a major challenge. Extreme poverty ravages the lives of one person in four in the developing world. Illiteracy, hunger and disease are still widespread, and HIV/AIDS has become a scourge in many developing countries. About half of the poor are children suffering from hardship, want and violence — and the majority of poor adults are women. Social and economic inequality within nations is an obstacle to sustainable poverty reduction. Globalisation offers promising avenues for spurring growth and reducing poverty, but special effort will be required to ensure that poor countries and poor people share adequately in its opportunities and benefits.

We are profoundly concerned with the plight of people living in severe poverty. Beyond our shared moral concerns for those less fortunate, we consider that reducing poverty and global inequalities is essential to our common interest, given the potential impact on regional and global security, international co-operation, sustainable development and prosperity. Developing countries must assume leadership and formulate effective national strategies for reducing poverty. These strategies should integrate economic, social, environmental and governance concerns within a comprehensive approach to development at the country level. We pledge to help them meet this challenge, in partnership with civil society, the private sector and multilateral institutions. We further pledge our best efforts to help developing countries address the challenges of globalisation and the digital age, and deal with HIV/AIDS and other killer diseases.

We confirm our commitment to reducing poverty in all its dimensions and to achieving the seven International Development Goals (IDGs). We view the IDGs in the context of the broader set of goals – including on hunger, safe water and HIV/AIDS – agreed in the Millennium Summit Declaration and in the context as well of the ultimate objective of poverty eradication.

The IDGs include: by 2015, halving extreme income poverty, lowering infant, child and maternal mortality, and ensuring universal primary education and access to reproductive health services; and by 2005, achieving gender parity in education as a step towards gender equality and the empowerment of women, and implementing strategies for sustainable development as a step towards reversing the loss of environmental resources.

We restate our determination to promote qualitative factors of development – including effective, democratic and accountable governance, the protection of human rights, and respect for the rule of law – in supporting partner country efforts to build stable, safe, participatory and just societies. We resolve to ensure centrality of sustainable poverty reduction in development co-operation, particularly at country level. We resolve also to enhance the coherence of our overall policies that impact on development including, for example, opening markets and implementing accelerated debt relief. We will intensify our efforts to increase the effectiveness of aid and mobilise additional resources for reducing poverty. In so doing, most Members are guided by the 0.7% ODA/GNP target.

We have developed *Guidelines on Poverty Reduction* in consultation with our international partners: the World Bank, the International Monetary Fund and the United Nations Development Programme. The Guidelines represent an emerging international consensus and a shared commitment and understanding of how to work together more effectively to help developing country partners reduce poverty. We agree on the following principles that underlie these Guidelines:

## Poverty is multidimensional

**We share a broad understanding of poverty and its many dimensions.**

Poverty encompasses different dimensions of deprivation that relate to human capabilities including consumption and food security, health, education, rights, voice, security, dignity and decent work. Poverty must be reduced in the context of environmental sustainability. Reducing gender inequality is key to all dimensions of poverty.

## The coherence of our policies matters

**We will strive to elevate policy coherence for poverty reduction as a general concern in government policies and develop the means necessary to promote it across our governments and in international fora.**

Reducing poverty requires better coherence in government policies affecting development. Key policy areas with potentially strong poverty reduction impact include debt relief, trade, investment, agriculture, the environment, migration, health research, security and arms sales.

## Economic growth: pace, quality and equity

Reducing poverty calls for rapid and sustainable pro-poor growth. This requires good governance, prudent macroeconomic management, competitive markets and a vibrant private sector, efficient institutions and sustainable use of natural resources. Making growth pro-poor requires equitable participation by poor men and women in generating and benefiting from growth. It also requires reforms to reduce inequalities regarding human capabilities and access to assets and productive resources such as land, training and credit.

**We will support partner efforts to promote sustainable pro-poor growth, reduce inequality and increase their shares of global trade and investment flows.**

## Reducing poverty calls for political will by all partners

Poverty reduction involves a political process. It requires dedicated efforts to empower the poor by strengthening their voice and fostering democratic accountability. Strategic partnerships with reform-minded forces within government and civil society can be helpful in fostering social and political transformation. Support for broader country dialogue and stakeholder participation must be consistent with partner efforts to build democratic institutions.

**We will support partner country efforts to engage civil society in setting priority poverty reduction goals and measures to reduce inequalities, consistent with their efforts to build democratic institutions.**

## Needs and performance will be key factors in aid allocations

Development co-operation resources must be used effectively for reducing poverty. Priority will be accorded to countries with low incomes. Some targeted assistance to other countries with a large proportion of poor people may also be provided. The level of political commitment to fight poverty and the effectiveness of government policies will be key considerations in this regard. At the same time, it is important to support the poor in countries with severe governance problems, including conflict-prone countries.

**We will give priority to poor countries with government commitment to reducing poverty and using aid effectively, but will also target aid, selectively, to poor people in countries with severe governance problems.**

## Supporting poverty reduction strategies of partner countries through different types of assistance

**We will increase the use of co-ordinated programme, sector and project assistance supporting the implementation of country-led strategies and programmes for reducing poverty.**

Development co-operation will support goals and priorities as set out in national strategies for sustainable poverty reduction, which should be country-driven, participatory, comprehensive and results-oriented. To ensure ownership and sustainability, the development community should be moving from agency-driven to country-led activities, creating space for partnership through integrated programme, project and sector-wide support. Key priorities for supporting the implementation of partner strategies include resources for capacity-building, institutional reform and broad participation of local partners.

## Better aid management for increased effectiveness

**We will undertake best efforts to work collaboratively, streamline our administrative requirements where possible, and co-ordinate our approaches and actions with those of our partners.**

Effective aid calls for improved aid co-ordination by working collaboratively, undertaking joint tasks, and combining skills and resources. While maintaining high standards of accountability and transparency, DAC Members can simplify and harmonise administrative and financial requirements, adjust to local procedures where these are adequate and help partners improve their administrative capacity and performance.

## Assessing performance

**We will assess our development co-operation efforts in terms of their effectiveness in promoting genuine partnership and their impact on reducing poverty.**

Strong partnerships are based on dialogue, mutual trust and joint accountability. Each partner should be assessed in terms of meeting agreed commitments and achieving poverty reduction impact. Development agencies should develop specific partnership performance goals, such as promoting country leadership, providing resources more flexibly, more predictably and over longer time frames, and ensuring that development assistance to the public sector is fully reflected in government budgets.

## Strengthening agency institutional alignment with poverty reduction, partnership and policy coherence goals

Integrating poverty reduction as a critical agency-wide concern, developing partnership capacity and promoting policy coherence are key institutional goals for development agencies. This will often call for changes and creative approaches to agency organisational structures, practices, incentive systems and cultures.

**We are committed to incorporating poverty reduction and partnership in the policies and operations of our agencies, and will undertake best efforts to adapt our institutional practices, systems and cultures accordingly.**

# Executive Summary

## Delivering on the global goals for reducing poverty: a call to action

For several decades the development assistance community has worked with the people and governments of developing countries to improve their living conditions. Progress – though often unrecognised – has been remarkable. In the past 30 years alone, life expectancy increased by more than 20 years (to 62). Infant mortality rates dropped by half. Primary school enrolment rates have doubled. Major developing countries, particularly in East Asia, have passed rapidly from low- to middle-income status.

These results are highly encouraging. They demonstrate that poverty *can* be overcome. But the battle is far from over. Extreme income poverty still ravages the lives of one in four persons (or 1.2 billion people) in the developing world[1] – one in five in the world at large – and progress in tackling it has been uneven. Although Asia has advanced rapidly, it still accounts for most of the world's poor. Sub-Saharan Africa has struggled with slow growth and rising poverty, partly linked to conflict and governance problems, and it now faces the scourge of HIV/AIDS.

Emerging threats loom large. Social and economic inequality within nations is an obstacle to sustainable poverty reduction. The marginalisation of ethnic and other minorities continues to trigger outbreaks of violent conflict. And poor people continue to be excluded from economic and political life in many countries and from the global mainstream. Both the challenges and the stakes for eradicating poverty are high – and they are rising.

Changing global dynamics are adding new and troubling dimensions to poverty. The accelerating pace of economic integration among nations will fuel future growth in incomes and jobs. It will stimulate new patterns of production and exchange. And it will create unprecedented opportunities for communicating, learning and sharing knowledge with others. Globalisation holds great promise for empowering people and for promoting greater international understanding, linkages and partnerships. But it also threatens to widen the divide between rich and poor, leaving some poor countries and regions increasingly behind. Globalisation will not deliver its potential benefits if it works for only a few.

At the same time, in a rapidly globalising world the social ills associated with poverty – disease, illicit migration, environmental degradation, crime, political instability, armed conflict and terrorism – can spread with greater ease across borders and continents. Compounding this are the pressures of population growth. Of the estimated increase of 2 billion people over the next 20 years, 97% will live in the developing world. Eradicating poverty is thus more than a moral and humanitarian imperative. It is also essential for global security and prosperity and for reducing environmental stresses. It is an international public good of the first order, serving the interests of all.

The current conjuncture for confronting poverty is promising. There is now broad global commitment to halving the proportion of people in extreme income poverty and hunger by 2015. Developing countries are establishing and implementing strategies to

*Tangible development progress has been achieved in the developing world through the combined efforts of governments, civil society and development assistance agencies...*

*... but extreme poverty still ravages the lives of one in four persons.*

*Eradicating poverty is essential for global security and prosperity...*

© OECD 2001

achieve this goal. And the international development community is putting together a co-ordinated and focused response, mustering the political will and establishing the frameworks and mechanisms for organising a more effective assault on poverty.

**... and thus everyone has a stake in working to reduce it.**

The time is right to seize the opportunities at hand: rising political will to tackle poverty, the potential of globalisation for all and technological advances in telecommunications, information and the life sciences. It is essential to deliver on promises, convictions and goals, following through with commitment, resources and well-founded efforts on the ground. Everyone has a stake in working more effectively, with greater scope, to reduce global poverty.

## Implementing the DAC 21st century strategy

The OECD/DAC strategy *Shaping the 21st Century: The Contribution of Development Co-operation* set out a vision of development co-operation based on partnership around development strategies owned and led by developing country governments and civil societies. The principles underpinning this vision – partnership, ownership, country leadership, broad-based participation, development effectiveness and accountability – have far-reaching implications for the way development agencies conduct business. Development co-operation agencies now need to work in a much closer, more co-ordinated way with a wider range of development partners.[2] They should tailor assistance to partner country priorities and needs where the conditions for partnership exist. They are now accountable to partners and to their own publics for actions and commitments. They need to work as facilitators – rather than prime movers – of development.

**Under the impetus of the OECD/DAC strategy "Shaping the 21st Century"...**

The 21st century strategy also committed DAC Members to support poverty reduction in developing countries by assisting them to achieve a limited set of goals for economic and social development and environmental sustainability – the International Development Goals (IDGs) – based on agreements at international fora in the 1990s. DAC Members also agreed to promote qualitative factors in the evolution of more stable, safe, participatory and just societies, which they considered essential to the attainment of these measurable goals. These include capacity development for effective, democratic and accountable governance, the protection of human rights and respect for the rule of law.

A broader set of quantitative and qualitative development goals for monitoring progress towards the ultimate objective of poverty eradication is included in the United Nations Millennium Declaration, adopted by heads of State and Government in September 2000. These measurable goals subsume and update the IDGs first set out in the OECD/DAC 21st century strategy. The Millennium Development Goals (MDGs)[3] are set out on next page.

**... bilateral agencies have developed this set of guidelines to help them work more effectively to reduce poverty.**

Under the impetus of the 21st century strategy, DAC Members are committing themselves to work with greater resolve to reduce poverty in solidarity with poor people and in the interests of securing universal human rights. They will be working to ensure centrality of sustainable poverty reduction in development co-operation and to integrate economic, social, environmental and governance concerns within comprehensive approaches to development at the country level.

Determined to work more effectively to reduce poverty, DAC Members have now developed a set of guidelines to help concert and improve their individual and collective efforts. The *DAC Guidelines on Poverty Reduction* cover five major themes: poverty concepts and approaches, partnership issues, country programming, policy coherence and institutional change in development agencies. This summary highlights key *Guidelines'* conclusions, commitments and challenges.

## Millennium Development Goals (MDGs)

### GOAL 1: Eradicate extreme poverty and hunger

**Target 1.** Halve, between 1990 and 2015, the proportion of people whose income is less than one dollar a day

**Target 2.** Halve, between 1990 and 2015, the proportion of people who suffer from hunger

### GOAL 2: Achieve universal primary education

**Target 3.** Ensure that, by 2015, children everywhere, boys and girls alike, will be able to complete a full course of primary schooling

### GOAL 3: Promote gender equality and empower women

**Target 4.** Eliminate gender disparity in primary and secondary education preferably by 2005 and to all levels of education no later than 2015

### GOAL 4: Reduce child mortality

**Target 5.** Reduce by two-thirds, between 1990 and 2015, the under-five mortality rate

### GOAL 5: Improve maternal health

**Target 6.** Reduce by three-quarters, between 1990 and 2015, the maternal mortality ratio

### GOAL 6: Combat HIV/AIDS, malaria and other diseases

**Target 7.** Have halted by 2015, and begun to reverse, the spread of HIV/AIDS

**Target 8.** Have halted by 2015, and begun to reverse, the incidence of malaria and other major diseases

### GOAL 7: Ensure environmental sustainability

**Target 9.** Integrate the principles of sustainable development into country policies and programmes and reverse the loss of environmental resources

**Target 10.** Halve, by 2015, the proportion of people without sustainable access to safe drinking water

**Target 11.** By 2020, have achieved a significant improvement in the lives of at least 100 million slum-dwellers

### GOAL 8: Develop a global partnership for development

**Target 12.** Develop further an open, rule-based, predictable, non-discriminatory trading and financial system Includes a commitment to good governance, development, and poverty reduction – both nationally and internationally

**Target 13.** Address the Special Needs of the Least Developed Countries Includes: tariff and quota free access for LDC exports; enhanced programme of debt relief for HIPC and cancellation of official bilateral debt; and more generous ODA for countries committed to poverty reduction

**Target 14.** Address the Special Needs of landlocked countries and small island developing states (through Barbados Programme and 22nd General Assembly provisions)

**Target 15.** Deal comprehensively with the debt problems of developing countries through national and international measures in order to make debt sustainable in the long term

**Target 16.** In co-operation with developing countries, develop and implement strategies for decent and productive work for youth

**Target 17.** In co-operation with pharmaceutical companies, provide access to affordable, essential drugs in developing countries

**Target 18.** In co-operation with the private sector, make available the benefits of new technologies, especially information and communications

---

**Box 1. The need for fast, pro-poor growth**

Vigorous, sustained economic growth in the private sector creates jobs and incomes for the poor. It also generates public revenues to finance social development and social protection programmes and to strengthen the institutional framework and physical infrastructure for efficient markets. The state, the private sector and civil society all have crucial roles in reducing poverty by fostering pro-poor economic growth through efficient and competitive markets. But even rapid and durable growth can leave people behind. Only about half the increase in incomes of the poorest fifth of the population comes from GDP growth. The other half comes from the *quality* of growth – from its composition, distribution and sustainability.

How to achieve more pro-poor growth? By adopting policies and programmes that enable poor people to access human, physical and financial assets that can increase their productivity and incomes, for example enhanced social services (particularly education and health), land tenure reform and micro-finance schemes. The development of smallholder farming and labour-intensive manufacturing as well as supportive infrastructure and institutions are also vital for pro-poor growth. Other key elements are, more broadly, good governance including prudent macroeconomic management with low inflation, and institutional capacity, including sound frameworks for financial markets and the corporate sector.

---

## Common concepts and approaches for understanding and addressing poverty

Sustainable poverty reduction calls for effective strategies based on clear and consistent concepts and approaches. Different ways of understanding poverty leads to different ways of dealing with it. A common and clear understanding of poverty helps build a common agenda with development partners, linking specific causes of poverty in each setting with suitable policies and actions. The following steps are basic for poverty reduction approaches in each country:

■ Identify the main causes of poverty.

■ Design and rank policies and actions that address these causes.

■ Specify the indicators or goals for monitoring progress.

■ Seek broad agreement on policies and programmes to tackle poverty.

**A shared understanding – among all development partners – of poverty and its many dimensions is crucial for working together.**

**Poverty is multidimensional.** Poverty denotes people's exclusion from socially adequate living standards and it encompasses a range of deprivations. The dimensions of poverty cover distinct aspects of human capabilities: economic (income, livelihoods, decent work), human (health, education), political (empowerment, rights, voice), socio-cultural (status, dignity) and protective (insecurity, risk, vulnerability). Mainstreaming gender is essential for reducing poverty in all its dimensions. And sustaining the natural resource base is essential for poverty reduction to endure.

**Causes of poverty vary widely from one country to another.** History, geography and governance all shape development patterns. Wars, armed conflicts and collapses of the state cause poverty and make it worse. Entrenched corruption, rent-seeking élites, lack of respect for human rights, inefficient bureaucracies and weak commitment to undertake policy and institutional reforms are all inimical to reducing poverty. Other important causes of poverty are environmental degradation, gender discrimination and rapid population growth. AIDS has now emerged as a critical poverty issue requiring wide-ranging action.

**The pace and quality of economic growth is a key aspect of a national strategy to reduce poverty.**

**Promoting pro-poor growth and reducing inequality.** Increasing economic growth rates is essential (Box 1) – but it is not enough. The quality of growth – its sustainability, composition and equity – is equally important. In many countries, inequalities in incomes and access to assets tend to undermine both the pace and quality of growth – and hence the effect of growth on poverty reduction. When inequality gives rise to conflict and violence, it has disastrous human and economic consequences. So, development agencies should make efforts to strengthen coalitions supporting reforms to reduce inequality.

**Empowering the poor.** Powerlessness, injustice and exclusion perpetuate poverty – and make it worse. The poor need to be able to exercise their human rights and to influence state institutions and social processes that affect their lives. Rights-based approaches to poverty reduction strengthen the norms and institutions that protect universal human rights (including those of children and workers) through open political, economic, legal and judicial systems. Key elements for empowering the poor include:

- Strengthening popular participation in formulating and implementing policy and in assessing impact.

- Promoting democratic and accountable governance and transparency.

- Promoting human rights and the rights of marginalised groups.

- Increasing the scope for civil society interaction and freedom of association.

- Supporting a free press.

- Reinforcing the rule of law and the impartial administration of justice.

- Promoting decent work conditions.

- Giving the poor more voice and control over the type, quality and delivery of services they receive.

**Basic social services.** The social progress objectives of human development call for adequate levels of health, education, water, sanitation and social protection. Social development, critical for poverty reduction, is a right in itself. It directly improves the lives of poor women and men, and contributes to overall growth and development. Education, especially for girls, and reproductive health services are crucial factors for defeating poverty and some of its major aspects – illness, including AIDS, unsafe motherhood, and high population growth. Disease and illiteracy are barriers to well-being and productive employment. Reading and writing facilitate communication with others, which is crucial in social and political participation. Public spending on social services is important, if used efficiently. It needs to be coupled with incentives and pro-poor financing methods, including social insurance, to ensure access, affordability and quality of services rendered. If the poor are to benefit, partner country governments need resources to invest in infrastructure and provide basic services. For some services, particularly water supply and sanitation, user fees or private sector involvement within a legal framework of social equity can improve access as well as management efficiency.

*Efforts to empower the poor to exercise their human rights and to have voice...*

*... to facilitate their access to basic social services...*

**... to strengthen their capacity to pursue sustainable livelihoods...**

**Sustainable livelihoods approaches – addressing the needs and capabilities of poor people.** These approaches start by asking poor women and men about their needs and notions and, based on this information, proceed by determining necessary policy reforms in the context of sustainable development. Poor people's sources of livelihood are highly varied, ranging from natural resources to handicrafts, trade and services. Sustainable livelihoods approaches involve institutional development to buttress the ability of poor people to overcome poverty, for example by sustained improvements of farm productivity and food security.

**... and to help them cope with risk and vulnerability are key in fighting poverty.**

**Human security: reducing vulnerability and managing shocks.** How do poor people see insecurity? As a major dimension of poverty. Promoting human security requires measures to protect people from disruptions to nations and households. It also requires addressing the many sources of risk that affect poor people – lack of food, ill health, unemployment, crime, old age, domestic violence, armed conflict, natural disaster and other environmental risks.

## Forging effective poverty reduction partnerships

**Development agencies should establish partnerships that facilitate and strengthen local ownership of development policies and activities.**

The new emphasis on partnerships for reducing poverty calls for a comprehensive rethinking of development co-operation practices. Six principles should govern agency actions:

- Partnership approaches, which facilitate and strengthen local ownership, should be the basis for all development assistance efforts.

- National ownership of poverty reduction strategies, including locally-determined policies and priorities, should consistently be respected, promoted and supported in all interactions with partners.

- Agency support for a national poverty reduction strategy should be based on a sound assessment of the merits, drawbacks and trade-offs of the strategy's approach.

- The active participation of a range of partners and the empowerment of the poor are vital.

- Better co-ordination and longer-term commitment can strengthen partnerships and increase impact.

- Development efforts should be monitored and evaluated with government partners and poor people themselves in order to assess partnership performance and to secure and maintain pro-poor effects.

**Partnerships call for mutual commitment and trust based on shared objectives and proven performance.**

**Sound, productive partnerships are based on trust, mutual accountability and a shared commitment to goals and objectives.** Partnerships work best when they are based on reciprocal relationships characterised by clear understandings about the roles and responsibilities of the different partners and where there is open, inclusive dialogue among them. To strengthen trust and commitment, partners need to assess each other's performance in meeting agreed responsibilities and obligations.

Measures of partner country performance could include:

- The scope and pace of government efforts to orient strategies in a pro-poor, gender-aware direction.

- The quality of the policy dialogue.

- The extent and quality of local consultative processes in developing national poverty reduction strategies.

- The impact of poverty reduction policies and programmes.

Similarly, the performance of development agencies could be assessed to determine whether:

■ Planning and implementation activities support country-led strategies, co-ordinated with other partners.

■ Agency activities respect and foster local ownership.

■ Resources are provided more flexibly and predictably.

■ Assistance, including specific projects, is being integrated in partner government expenditure frameworks.

■ Agency support has had an impact on reducing poverty.

**Marshall all potential development partners to ensure ownership, sustainability and effectiveness.** Civil society, the private sector, parliaments, local government, trade unions, poor people, external agencies – all should participate in designing and implementing strategies for reducing poverty. This diversity of actors demands better communication, reinforced by strong co-operation, and a good understanding of the relative strengths and comparative advantages of each of them. Development agencies can play an important role in strengthening the capacity of civil society to engage with government and in supporting consultation mechanisms. Due consideration should be given to the scope for non-governmental organisations, chambers of commerce and the enterprise sector to spearhead effective and innovative initiatives for reducing poverty.

*Civil society participation in dialogue on development strategies and options should be actively supported.*

**Partnership means dialogue with and beyond government.** A broad range of partners should be engaged in the policy dialogue process when poverty reduction strategies are devised. Extra effort will be required to ensure that, from the beginning, *genuine participation informing policy decisions and outcomes takes place* in these consultations. This means promoting local democratic structures and identifying civil society actors who can legitimately speak for the poor and be accountable to them. It also means taking care not to undermine the legitimacy of partner governments – instead respecting what partners are doing to build and consolidate their constitutional and democratic institutions.

**Allocate resources for effective poverty reduction.** Given the limited volumes of development assistance and the importance of reducing poverty, it is vital that development co-operation resources are used as effectively as possible. Country allocation criteria need to take into account both the number and proportion of very poor people and include an assessment of the scope for the effectiveness of aid in a given partner country. Maximising the impact of development co-operation on reducing poverty implies:

■ Concentration on the poorest countries, although some targeted funding should also be provided to other developing countries with widespread poverty.

■ More emphasis on medium- and larger-sized countries, where the vast majority of the very poor are found, although aid per capita would remain significantly higher in smaller countries.

■ Taking account of aid effectiveness factors drawn from DAC experience that highlight the importance of both political commitment to fight poverty and an effective policy and institutional environment.

■ Ensuring that the partner country's poverty reduction strategy is legitimate, adequate and appropriate.

**Helping partners in severe difficulty.** Aid is often provided to address development objectives such as conflict prevention, human rights and participatory democracy, gender equality and sustainable development. There is also often an acute need to help countries adjust to external shocks, for example refugees fleeing conflict in neighbouring countries, natural disasters, or terms-of-trade shocks – all of which affect economic and social development performance.

**Collaborate closely with other external partners in dealing with dilemma situations.** Countries with inadequate development policies and institutions need support to create conditions enabling performance to improve. Working as partners with such countries in ways that promote country ownership – and yet that ensure aid is effective and has poverty reduction impact – is likely to be problematical. What happens when a partner government does not comply, or only partially complies, with its stated intentions or commitments? Policy conditions – often bundled with financial and technical support – have sometimes helped reform-minded (usually new) governments advance reform agendas. But externally-imposed conditionality has generally not been effective, sustainable or conducive to country ownership and is least likely to work in countries lacking the basis for partnership. Emerging good practice suggests the following approaches:

- A moderate share of assistance should be reserved for these countries.

- External partners should have a shared view of the partner country and co-ordinate their development co-operation and other actions and policies.

- Assistance should be used to support sustainable national or local institutions and civil society, with an emphasis on addressing the barriers to adequate performance such as promoting renewed policy dialogue, supporting local coalitions for reform and strengthening local capacity for research and social dialogue.

- Development co-operation could also support local authorities and non-governmental organisations (NGOs) in relieving poverty among targeted populations to reduce vulnerability and to satisfy humanitarian needs.

**Reducing poverty involves a political process.** Pro-poor structural and policy reforms in partner countries often raise difficult political issues. Some groups are clinging to power, privileges and rents. Others are more amenable to pursuing reform and implementing pro-poor policies. Development agencies are understandably reluctant to be involved in sensitive internal political issues, but cannot ignore these tensions. By supporting government efforts to engage society in dialogue on development options and choices, agencies will be able to understand more about local social and political dynamics and to build strategic alliances and partnerships with reform-minded groups and institutions. Encouraging pluralistic, participatory democracies that give voice to the poor can also address this challenge.

**Aid co-ordination is the joint responsibility of all partners, although it should be initiated and led by partner governments.** External agencies should undertake more disciplined and sustained efforts to work with one another to assure coherent approaches and a strong focus on fundamental needs and collaboration opportunities. They need to share more information with others to ensure genuine co-ordination and enable other local and external partners to use their frameworks to fullest advantage. The challenge for the development community is to find ways of collaborating that do not undermine country ownership nor create an extra burden for partner countries.

**Closer collaboration with multilateral and regional institutions is key.** There are four practical steps involved in working more effectively with these agencies. First, initiate early and continuous contact with relevant multilateral staff. Second, agree on the respective roles, responsibilities and obligations of different external partners in country-specific poverty reduction strategy processes. Third, keep periodic co-ordination meetings informal, operational and focused on results. Fourth, where feasible, streamline and simplify funding and disbursement arrangements.

---

## Box 2.  An action agenda for the bilateral community

The *Guidelines* set out the following priorities for bilateral agencies working with partners to reduce poverty:

■ Support country-owned, country-led strategies for reducing poverty, and base agency programming on needs and priorities identified in these strategies.

■ Allocate more development assistance to countries where there is greatest scope for reducing poverty given the number of absolute poor, the strength of government commitment to tackle poverty and demonstrated policy performance. Reserve funding for countries dealing with external shocks or conflict situations, and for countries with very weak development policies.

■ Reduce the burden that development co-operation creates for local partners by combining efforts (for example, joint missions, collaborative research, common diagnostics, shared costs, etc.), easing administrative requirements (for example, simplifying, streamlining and harmonising paperwork and procedures and accepting partner design for strategies and documents wherever possible), and co-ordinating agency approaches and actions.

■ Invest the time and resources needed to build genuine, reciprocal, poverty reduction partnerships.

■ Adapt agency structures and working methods to the challenges and needs of poverty reduction partnerships

(for example, strengthen field presence; enhance field-level decision-making flexibility; develop staff "facilitation" and consensus-building skills; increase transparency and accountability to other partners).

■ Work more intensively to develop human and institutional capacity in partner countries.

■ Ensure a gender perspective in all policies, programmes and instruments.

■ Integrate sustainable development, including environmental concerns, into strategic frameworks for reducing poverty.

■ Adopt, to the greatest extent possible, a multi-year timeframe for poverty reduction programming and funding as a complement to multi-year partner government fiscal planning and budgeting.

■ Assess development co-operation for its impact on poverty and develop the requisite monitoring and evaluation systems and methodologies.

■ Foster and strengthen local capacities to monitor poverty reduction programmes and the use of external and domestic resources in the context of debt relief programmes.

■ Encourage the development of local poverty reduction indicators and targets – and strengthen local statistical, analytical, monitoring and evaluation capacity.

---

## Frameworks and instruments for country programming

To translate their poverty reduction objectives into more effective programmes, agencies should use partner country strategic frameworks, a judicious mix of aid instruments and proven best practices.

**Agency programmes should, first and foremost, build on partner country development frameworks.**  In their various national adaptations, the planning frameworks promoted by the international community (such as the PRSP, NSSD, CDF, and UNDAF/CCA[4]) are strategic for translating the Millennium Development Goals into national policy and action. But these closely related, often interlocking frameworks must be rationalised to reduce the burden of having partner countries comply with multiple planning instruments. Ideally, the frameworks should coalesce into a single, comprehensive national strategy for reducing poverty that integrates economic, social and environmental priorities.

*Agency support for poverty reduction should be based on the partner country's national development strategy.*

**The emerging national poverty reduction strategies should be the point of departure for external assistance.**  These strategies should be country-driven, participatory, comprehensive and results-oriented. Agencies should tolerate different formats and standards. They should be aware of – and accommodate – often over-stretched country capacity, and allow time for local ownership to grow. They should set realistic targets, taking into account local capacity to implement strategies and recognising that sustained poverty reduction cannot be achieved overnight.

**Agencies need to sharpen the poverty focus and impact of country programmes.**  Consistent with the trend in partner countries to develop poverty reduction strategies, agency country programmes should focus primarily on the poverty reduction goals identified by the partner country. Agencies can play a crucial role in promoting informed local policy formulation processes by sharing information, analysis, diagnostic studies, user surveys, data, and other knowledge with local partners. Programmes should reflect the best knowledge of poverty in the country. And taking into consideration what other development agencies are doing in the country, they should reflect the agency's comparative advantage.

**Using a variety of aid instruments – programme, project and sector support – fosters synergies and complementarities.**

**Country programming should consist of a mix of aid instruments, drawing on synergies.** The instruments include financial support for national, regional and sectoral programmes and projects. These are often used in combination with policy dialogue, underpinned by technical co-operation which is frequently integrated with the relevant project or programme. Each instrument has its advantages and drawbacks, depending on the partner country. But to ensure ownership and sustainability, the development community should move from agency-driven activities to co-operation modes in support of partner-led programmes. This implies attention to programme aid and sector support, but there is also much that can be done through projects, all co-ordinated in support of partner leadership. The choice of instruments and the balance between indirect and focused actions should flow from an analysis of the country's needs elicited through a dialogue with government and other stakeholders.

**Programme aid opens the way to a continuing dialogue on pro-poor policies.** Programme support allows financial resources to be disbursed with minimum transaction costs. By giving the partner country fuller responsibility for financial decisions and management, such support underpins the principles of partnership and ownership. In the right political, economic and institutional environment, programme aid supporting a sound poverty reduction strategy is likely to have the biggest impact. But given the fungibility of resources, it is important to ensure that programme aid supports a sound, agreed and monitored reform programme. Debt relief, which *de facto* provides programme-type assistance, is based on similar principles.

**Sector support holds potential for shifting attention to poverty and inequality.** Sector programmes, including sector-wide approaches, can enhance local ownership, strengthen partnership and establish an institutional environment conducive to reducing poverty. To exploit the advantages of the emerging sector-wide approaches for reducing poverty, agencies need to address multiple challenges. They must accept locally-owned sector strategies and promote a more focused dialogue on equity in social development, particularly in the crucial sectors of health and education. They should elevate rights of the poor and issues of gender as primary concerns in specific sectors. They should give priority to building local capacity to formulate policies and implement programmes. They should involve civil society and foster partnerships with the private sector. And they should rationalise accounting and reporting procedures. Extending this kind of support also hinges on the partner country's ability to comply with required standards of accountability and financial governance regarding the use of external funds.

**Partner-led projects can make a lasting impact on the livelihoods and well-being of beneficiaries.** Projects addressing poverty will have greatest impact when they are embedded within a broader development framework, such as the national poverty reduction strategy or a sector programme. When they promote ownership and participation, rely on local knowledge and focus on increasing capacities, they have greater potential for making a sustainable contribution to poverty reduction. Projects should be compatible with the surrounding institutional and cultural environment and be accepted by central government, local authorities and civil society. Agencies should avoid small projects affecting a limited amount of people that place disproportionate burdens on scarce partner capacity. They should also move away from top-down micro-management in both design and implementation, which results in lack of sustainability after the withdrawal of external funding.

**Strengthening partners' own capacities to reduce poverty should be an overriding objective for technical co-operation.** Technical co-operation for capacity-building, either free-standing or embedded in other projects or sector-wide approaches, has an important and continuing role to play. To increase its impact, development agencies should apply well-tested good practices. First, set self-reliance and the principle of minimum intervention as a strategic objective, rather than use technical co-operation to get tasks accomplished or fill gaps in local competence. Second, plan technical co-operation in the context of national poverty reduction strategies and sector programmes, rather than make isolated, donor-driven proposals. Third, define objectives as outcomes to be achieved rather than inputs to be provided. Fourth, promote the capacity of local experts and provide for transfer of know-how by international experts where needed. Fifth, as in the case of project and much sectoral assistance, strengthen existing institutions and capacities, both public and private, including universities, rather than promote parallel structures. And sixth, ensure that recurrent costs are sustainable and will be picked up in national or local budgets. These good practices apply to financial co-operation as well.

Finally, other instruments of rising importance in agency portfolios such as debt relief, humanitarian aid and support for regional co-operation can be vital for poverty reduction.

## Policy coherence matters

**Reducing poverty requires coherence** – not only in development co-operation but also across OECD government policies – to avoid having the policies and actions of other parts of their governments undercut development agencies' efforts to reduce poverty. Such policy coherence for global poverty reduction should be elevated to each Member's national agenda. Indeed, government policies other than development co-operation may be more important for reducing poverty in developing countries. Consider agricultural and manufacturing tariffs and subsidies in industrialised countries: estimates suggest that they cause annual losses to developing countries of the same magnitude as annual flows of official development assistance. If non-tariff barriers and the regulation of trade-related services and intellectual property rights are included, then the estimate of losses may even triple.

**Policies across OECD Member governments should be coherent with the international poverty reduction goal.**

**Policy coherence is a profound political challenge.** Governments have a wide range of objectives reflecting domestic constituencies and interests. Even so, poverty reduction might now receive more weight in relation to other national objectives and become a higher priority for a broader range of policy-makers. Why? Because poverty is a source of dysfunction and disorder in the world – with adverse spillovers to political instability, terrorism, environmental degradation, illicit migration, epidemics and other international problems.

**Key steps for enhancing policy coherence.** The highest political authorities need to communicate their commitment to reduce global poverty throughout government, and to take measures to improve policy co-ordination to enhance coherence. Almost all DAC Members have made strong public commitments to reduce poverty. The challenge is to get this translated government-wide and used as a reference point when formulating and implementing policies. The most important policy areas are international trade and investment, agriculture and food security, natural resources and the environment, social issues, governance and human security.

**Key policy coherence areas for poverty reduction include trade, agriculture, food security, conflict prevention and social issues.**

**Making policies coherent across government is a complex process.** But there are ways in which much can be achieved. Examples are establishing a political mechanism, such as an interagency working group, for exchange and consultation within and across government ministries and departments; developing a government-wide policy brief on poverty reduction; systematically vetting legislation for its coherence with reducing poverty, and establishing cross-ministerial task forces for emerging issues, such as conflict prevention.

---

**Box 3.  An illustrative checklist on policy coherence for poverty reduction**

In the year 2000, the OECD Ministerial Council and the DAC High Level Meeting decided to develop a checklist for policy coherence that could be a reference point for public policies in Member countries. A checklist is included in the *Guidelines*. It covers a range of issues that impact on development. The checklist is illustrative rather than definitive, and serves to encourage Member governments systematically to integrate development and poverty issues into all relevant policy areas. It has been elaborated after consultations with a wide range of policy experts in the OECD. It is designed as a compact standalone reference document to be used by different policy communities in Member governments, and also to promote and guide further work within the OECD itself on policy coherence issues.

---

**Development agencies have an important role** – as advocates for development objectives and for ensuring that mechanisms exist for achieving policy coherence in practice. These mechanisms for policy coherence would apply, of course, to both development and other national objectives. Formal sessions are an invaluable tool for improving coherence, but a culture of informal contact is also critical.

## Changing the way we think and act

Agencies should consider how they will address institutional changes needed if the traditional *donor-recipient* relationship is to be reconstructed to one based on partnership, led by the developing country government's own priorities, and facilitated through shared knowledge and policy dialogue. This may well call for important changes in their organisational structures, practices, incentive systems and cultures. A successful change agenda will address the following issues:

### What is needed to mainstream poverty reduction throughout development agency operations?

**Working as partners will call for important changes...**

■ Determined leadership at both political and policy-making levels should capture and channel the *interest and commitment* of all staff, other government bodies and civil society to focus more resolutely and forcefully on supporting the poverty reduction efforts of partner countries. *There must also be a clear agency vision, policy framework and strategy* for helping partners reduce poverty, including country programming, sector approaches and project interventions. The goal of reducing poverty should inform all relevant agency planning processes and be a criterion in programme and project screening procedures.

**... in the way agencies are led and managed...**

■ The multidimensional approach to poverty reduction highlights the need to consider *reconfiguring organisational structures to facilitate better co-ordination and cross-fertilisation of expertise* and the exchange of knowledge within agencies. Good practice in this combines two approaches: making all staff responsible for promoting poverty reduction, and appointing poverty reduction "focal points" or "champions" to propel action and institutional change and learning. These focal points will need resources and authority to be effective.

**... and in organisational systems, structures, practices and cultures.**

■ *Agencies will need staff with broader ranges of specialist skills* (including the capacity to integrate the important cross-cutting concerns of gender, governance, environment and participatory approaches). They will have to provide specialist skills on poverty to field offices (including some with macroeconomic and technical skills). This can be done through agency staff who are resident in-country or in regional centres, supplemented by support from central agency staff. Training programmes dealing with poverty reduction issues and techniques will be needed to develop staff capacity to respond with wisdom and perspective.

---

■ *Mainstreaming also calls for encouraging team-work across professional boundaries* to address more effectively the multidimensional nature of poverty and to overcome sector-driven, supply-led approaches. This will have implications for the way agencies deploy and manage staff.

### How can agencies work more effectively with diverse partners under government leadership in the field?

■ Reducing the burden created by multiple administrative and financial requirements and improving agency co-ordination of policies and activities is very important. Efforts should focus on streamlining, simplifying and harmonising practices, procedures and reporting requirements in line with agency accountability requirements. Supporting the development of local capacity for accountability and transparency (financial management, accounting, monitoring) will strengthen agency confidence levels and facilitate moves towards aligning agency systems and procedures with those of developing country partners. This capacity-building need not be done by each individual agency, but through co-ordinated assistance among them.

**Simplifying agency reporting and accountability requirements and decentralising staff resources and decision-making to the field will facilitate partnership relations.**

■ Agencies also need to strengthen their institutional capacity to support partner governments in elaborating their own poverty reduction strategies and in interacting more effectively with other partners and stakeholders. This may require a change in agency attitudes and behaviour towards the role of civil society in policy formulation processes. Members should be realistic about the time required to generate broad-based support for strategies to reduce poverty and the resources this involves for partner governments, especially where capacity is weak.

■ Decentralising staff resources and decision-making to the field can help in several ways. It can improve understanding of local poverty conditions and heighten responsiveness to changing local circumstances. And it can strengthen team-work across disciplines and promote better dialogue and partnership through close and continuous interaction with other local partners.

■ Decentralisation decisions will have to balance these benefits against potential downside factors, such as increased costs and overstretched or excessively dispersed institutional technical expertise. Moreover, increased decentralisation is not necessarily a feasible and/or appropriate solution for smaller development assistance agencies, given associated additional costs and the extra efforts required to assure the quality of local programming and accountability. This argues all the more strongly for increasing collaboration and sharing expertise and information among all agencies, and for greater reliance on local expertise.

### How can agencies strengthen staff capacities and motivation to work in partnership?

■ *Management should stress the development of skills that foster partnership* (in facilitation, diplomacy, negotiation, co-ordination experience) and create opportunities for staff exchange, learning and team-work.

**Partnership reflexes and attitudes in agency staff can be cultivated through training and recruitment and appropriate agency reward and incentive systems.**

■ Staff recruitment and incentive structures (for permanent, temporary and diplomatic staff) should include a strong focus on poverty reduction and pro-poor growth skills and performance, team-work capacities, and efforts to initiate and sustain co-ordination with other staff and partners.

### How can organisational structures and practices promote better policy coherence across Member governments?

■ Efforts to improve policy coherence call for creating or improving mechanisms *to resolve contradictions or to mitigate the effects of conflicting government policies*. It also calls for a commitment of staff time and resources to identify and analyse issues and to interact in different national and global forums. Closer, more coherent interaction between agencies and other parts of their governments in dealing with multilateral institutions is one key to enhancing the broader coherence of development co-operation efforts.

## Achieving our goals

Focused development co-operation and greater policy coherence can do much to reduce poverty in developing countries. Yet impact will be modest without the initiative, efforts and resources of other partners, including partner governments, civil society, the private sector – and particularly the poor themselves. Achieving the goals will require a coalition of all forces. These *Guidelines* provide information, experience and shared orientations to assist bilateral agencies as they work with partner countries, with one another and with multilateral institutions in increasingly co-ordinated and collegial ways. All partners in development must strive together to ensure that progress in this new century is truly partner-driven and inclusive of all.

# Notes

1.  As measured by the international standard of US$1 (Purchasing Power Parity – PPP) per day. This figure would be 2.8 billion people, or 60% of the developing world, when using the US$2 per day standard.

2.  In this text, developing countries are referred to as "partner countries" or "partner governments", as opposed to "recipients", to indicate the importance attached to partnership processes and modalities. Similarly, the bilateral assistance community is referred to as "development agencies" or "agencies" (and not "donors"). "Stakeholders" refers to those who have an interest in reducing poverty.

3.  This formulation is subject to approval by the UN General Assembly in 2001 as part of its consideration of annual reporting on the Millennium Declaration.

4.  PRSP: Poverty Reduction Strategy Paper; NSSD: National Strategy for Sustainable Development; CDF: World Bank Comprehensive Development Framework; UNDAF/CCA: United Nations Development Assistance Framework/Common Country Assessment.

# General Introduction

## Poverty in a global perspective

Remarkable economic and social progress has taken place in the developing world over the past 30 years. Life expectancy has increased by more than 20 years (from 41 to 62) over this period. Infant mortality rates have been halved and primary school enrolment rates have doubled. The share of rural families with access to safe water has risen from 10% to more than 70%. Average incomes, health and literacy improved more in developing countries in these 30 years than they did in OECD countries in the past century.

But income poverty remains a challenge. Although the proportion of people in extreme poverty in developing and transition countries fell slightly over the past decade, from 28% to 24%, the numbers of poor people steadily increased in most regions (except for East Asia). And extremely poor people continue to be heavily concentrated in South Asia, which has the largest number of the world's poor (43% of the total), and in Africa, which has the highest proportion of its population living in poverty (48%).

Today extreme poverty ravages the lives of one in every four people (or 1.2 billion) in the developing world.[1] Poverty continues to be pervasive, intractable, inexcusable. In the last 10 years alone, the number of poor people in sub-Saharan Africa rose by more than a third. One in every three children in developing countries is unable to complete five years of education – the minimum required for basic literacy. One in every 12 children born this year will die of disease or malnutrition before her or his fifth birthday. And HIV/AIDS continues its relentless spread, erasing decades of development progress and exacting immense and tragic costs from children, families, communities and societies across the developing world. Strong and decisive action is needed to improve these statistics, particularly in view of the additional challenges posed by the 2 billion people – 97% of the expected increase in the world's population – projected to be born in developing countries over the next 25 years.

Robust, broad-based growth and improved access to social services will be key factors in reducing poverty. But progress will also depend on success in reducing inequalities. While the developing world as a whole experienced reasonable economic growth during the 1990s (on average 2.6% per capita), the total number of poor remained the same. Why? Because overall inequalities increased, particularly between countries, but also within countries, where gender is an important dimension explaining widening disparities. The UN estimates that women account for close to 70% of the world's poorest people and some social indicators show a strong gender bias. For example, young and adult women's illiteracy is nearly twice that of men, and child mortality rates are 28% higher for girls than for boys. Progress in reducing poverty involves tackling inequality, since poverty is falling much more rapidly with economic growth where inequality is lower.[2]

The progress achieved over previous decades gives one confidence that poverty can be overcome and development achieved. And yet, there is no cause for complacency. Eradicating poverty will call for sustained, adequately resourced and co-ordinated actions across the full spectrum of government policies and development co-operation activities. It will also call for the best efforts of all development partners. The Development Assistance Committee *Guidelines on Poverty Reduction,* which distil the accumulated

**Remarkable progress in economic development and well-being has been accomplished in developing countries over the past half century...**

**... but poverty continues to be pervasive, intractable – and inexcusable.**

**Robust economic growth, better access to essential public services and reduced inequalities – in particular as regards gender – are key factors for reducing poverty...**

**... as are sustained, adequately resourced and co-ordinated actions across government policies and development co-operation activities.**

knowledge and experience of the development community in addressing poverty reduction, are intended to inform these efforts and point the way ahead.

## A renewed commitment throughout the international system to fighting poverty

In 1996, OECD development ministers adopted a path-breaking policy framework for development co-operation. The OECD/DAC strategy *Shaping the 21st Century: The Contribution of Development Co-operation* set out a vision of development co-operation based on partnership around development strategies owned and led by developing country governments and civil societies. It also committed DAC Members to work with their partners towards achieving explicit, quantifiable and time-bound development goals based on economic, environmental and social development goals – which address many of the key dimensions of poverty – agreed upon by the international community during the UN-sponsored global conferences of the 1990s. Subsequently, this vision was reaffirmed by DAC Members in their May 2000 statement *Partnership for Poverty Reduction: From Commitment to Implementation*. The international development goals have been incorporated into the broader set of Millennium Development Goals – including on hunger, safe water, HIV/AIDS, slums and a global partnership for development – agreed in the UN Millennium Summit Declaration in 2000.[3] As an important step in implementing the 21st century strategy, DAC Members have synthesised their collective knowledge and expertise in dealing with poverty in this set of *Guidelines*.

In developing this guidance, DAC Members sought to put partnership into practice by sharing texts with a broad cross-section of poverty experts from government, civil society and academia in a series of consultations held in Africa, Asia, Latin America and Europe. The insights, concerns and views emanating from these exchanges have shaped the contents of the *Guidelines* and, in particular, the ideas and recommendations they contain for working as partners with other development actors.

The *Guidelines* set out a challenging agenda for the partnership era, calling for changes in the way development agencies[4] think about poverty, plan and implement related assistance, organise themselves in the field and at headquarters, and strengthen internal capacities to respond more effectively to the tasks at hand. At the same time, in setting out the rights, responsibilities and obligations implicit in partnership approaches, the *Guidelines* go far in fleshing out the substance and delimiting the boundaries of the emerging development partnerships model first described in *Shaping the 21st Century*.

## An overview of the DAC Guidelines on Poverty Reduction

These *Guidelines* are intended to help development agencies put poverty reduction at the centre of their policies and to operationalise these policies in the field. They clarify concepts and definitions, suggest priorities, and describe best practice in policies, programmes, instruments and channels for reducing poverty. They set out new directions in a number of areas, including:

■ **Common concepts and approaches for understanding, measuring, and focusing on poverty.** The *Guidelines* start by setting out a functional overview of poverty concepts and approaches and developing a framework for thinking about and understanding the nature and causes of poverty. They aim to help the reader grasp the multidimensional nature of poverty, who the poor are and ways in which anti-poverty measures can be shaped, combined and monitored.

■ **Forging poverty reduction partnerships.** A crucial challenge for the development community is the need to align development agency support squarely behind poverty reduction and partner government leadership. Part 2 of the *Guidelines* discusses how agencies can co-operate with others in building strong partnerships in diverse country situations and supporting national efforts to devise sound strategies for reducing poverty.

■ **Effective country programming, frameworks and instruments.** Part 3 discusses practical ways of working in partnership, focusing more closely on existing frameworks for organising and implementing development co-operation. It discusses the merits and challenges of a wide array of instruments and effective approaches in light of evolving practice and prospects for reducing poverty.

■ **Ensuring that the full range of DAC Members' policies are coherent with the objective of poverty reduction.** Policy coherence across Member governments (for example, trade, agriculture and environmental policies) is crucial to ensure that Members' efforts to reduce poverty are not undermined by the policies and actions of other parts of government. Part 4 deals with coherence at the national level between aid and non-aid policies and with coherence at the international level involving regional and global co-operation.

■ **Institutional learning and change.** The DAC 21st century strategy is creating a strong impetus for development agencies to transform the way they conduct business in accordance with the principles of partnership, ownership and accountability. The final section of the *Guidelines* focuses on the inner workings of development agencies, examining how organisational structures, management practices, and institutional cultures can be changed to increase their capacity to contribute effectively to reducing poverty.

While the *Guidelines* specifically address the concerns and functioning of the OECD bilateral development assistance community, their practical information and insights into how development partners can work together to reduce poverty are of value to all development practitioners.

## The role and purpose of the Guidelines

The *DAC Guidelines on Poverty Reduction* are designed to enable bilateral development agencies to help their partners in the developing world to address poverty. They signal a unity of purpose and commitment among DAC Members to work with greater resolve to reduce poverty in solidarity with poor people and in the interests of securing universal human rights.

In endorsing the *Guidelines*, Members resolve to ensure centrality of sustainable poverty reduction in development co-operation. An increasing number of DAC Members consider that the overarching goal of development co-operation should be to reduce and then eradicate poverty in the context of sustainable development. This requires the integration of economic, social, environmental and governance concerns within comprehensive approaches to development at the country level. Adoption of the *Guidelines* also means Members adopt a common view and understanding of poverty and appropriate approaches, frameworks and priorities for combating it. Their efforts will consequently be more coherent and mutually reinforcing, both among DAC Members and across the international system, given the full compatibility of the *Guidelines* with similar international frameworks.

**DAC Members are committed to addressing poverty through the integration of economic, social, environmental and governance concerns in a comprehensive approach to development.**

DAC Members also undertake to apply the principles of the *Guidelines* to their own work, for example in using partner country poverty reduction strategies as the basis for their bilateral programming, in reducing the burden that their procedures and requirements create for partner countries, and by improving policy coherence within and across their agencies and governments. They also agree to strive, so far as institutional opportunities and constraints permit, to implement recommendations, such as providing assistance more flexibly and predictably, creating favourable conditions for decentralising decision-making to the field, working through partner country planning frameworks, and ensuring that forms of support – whether programme or project aid – reflect local needs and constraints as regards recurrent cost financing, skills and environmental impacts.

**Each DAC Member has unique capacities, expertise and resources to contribute to the fight against poverty.**

DAC Members recognise the diversity of strengths and resources each of them can bring to the fight against poverty and the value of responding flexibly and creatively to needs and priorities as determined by partner governments and stakeholders. They agree on the continued importance of vibrant private sectors for jobs and incomes, of sustainable development for reversing environmental degradation, of good governance for promoting inclusion and participation, and of institution-building for developing local capacity and administrative systems. While these broader aspects of development co-operation are covered more completely in other DAC guidelines, Members note their potential role in reducing poverty and agree to work towards integrating poverty concerns and dimensions when formulating policies in these areas.

Adoption of the *Guidelines* also signals important messages about how the development co-operation community views emerging challenges – in the world at large and, more narrowly, within their own organisations – that have growing significance for the fight against poverty. This includes focused and committed efforts to explore new opportunities for reducing poverty; to address imbalances and needs arising from globalisation, global public goods and the digital divide; and to align their own institutional structures and cultures with the requisites of partnerships.

## How to use the Guidelines

The *Guidelines* provide practical information about the nature of poverty and how it is best tackled. They are thus of value to bilateral agency operational staff in the field and at headquarters. They also provide guidance on how to create appropriate policies and set priorities, how to work with different partners in developing countries and the international system, and how bilateral agencies could best be directed, reconfigured and retooled to work in partnership and to mainstream poverty reduction effectively. This information is of use to bilateral agency leadership, operational managers, and policy and human resource staff.

At the same time, given space constraints and the vastness of the subject at hand, the *Guidelines* remain broad and generic. The DAC will deepen their scope and substance by exploring key aspects of poverty reduction strategies and developing additional good practice.

**There is much to learn from one another, including by listening to – and heeding – the voices of the poor themselves.**

While considerable effort has been expended to ensure the *Guidelines* reflect contemporary research, knowledge and experience, they are not the last word. Indeed, in many respects – such as in promoting empowerment, better governance, participation and institution-building – development practitioners are at the incipient stage of knowing how best to act, and to interact, to reduce poverty. Further, each partner country is different and unique, defying a "one size fits all" approach to poverty reduction. There is still much to learn about good practice in this evolving area of development co-operation, including from listening to – and heeding – the voices of the poor themselves.

# Notes

1. This figure rises to 2.8 billion, or six out of every ten persons, if an international standard of US$2 per day is used.

2. *Global Economic Prospects and the Developing Countries*, World Bank, 2001, page ix. Martin Ravallion: *Growth, Inequality and Poverty: Looking Beyond Averages*, World Bank, 2000.

3. See the list of Millennium Development Goals, page 17.

4. These *Guidelines* refer to the bilateral assistance community as "development agencies" or "agencies", as opposed to "donors", a term inconsistent with partnership processes and modalities. Similarly, developing countries are referred to as "partner countries" or "partner governments" (not as "recipients"). "Stakeholders" in the text refers to developing country civil societies.

# 1 Concepts and Approaches

## Introduction

Effective poverty reduction calls for strategic thinking based on clear and consistent concepts and approaches. Different ways of understanding poverty lead to different ways of dealing with it. A common and clear understanding of poverty helps to build a common agenda with development partners. This first part of the *Guidelines* presents current notions of poverty and well-being in a conceptual framework that links the goal of sustainable poverty reduction with key causes of poverty and suitable policies and actions.[1]

**Clear concepts,...**

A strategic approach to poverty reduction mainly involves five analytical stages:

**... consistent policy approaches...**

*i.* **What is poverty?** – Clarifying and defining the concept.

*ii.* **Who are the poor?** – Identifying poverty lines and social categories.

*iii.* **How can poverty be measured and monitored?** – Choosing methods and indicators.

*iv.* **Why does poverty persist?** – Analysing structural and dynamic causes.

*v.* **Which policy actions are required?** – Formulating policies and programmes.

Development agencies need to think about these questions and produce answers based on experience and evidence. And they need to do it in partnership with other organisations that work towards poverty reduction, that is, government departments at all levels, other bilateral or multilateral agencies, and civil society organisations.

**... and partnerships are basic elements of poverty reduction strategies.**

## What is poverty?

### The widening meaning of poverty

The concept of poverty includes different dimensions of deprivation. In general, it is the inability of people to meet economic, social and other standards of well-being. The multidimensionality of poverty is now widely accepted. It is based solidly on research that includes major participatory studies of what poor people mean by poverty. It covers measures of *absolute poverty* such as child and infant mortality rates, and *relative poverty,* as defined by the differing standards of each society.[2]

The 1995 World Summit for Social Development in Copenhagen and the Millennium Development Goals both assumed that poverty is multidimensional. Similarly, the World Bank has defined poverty as unacceptable human deprivation in terms of economic opportunity, education, health and nutrition, as well as lack of empowerment and security. The United Nations Development Programme (UNDP) has introduced two relevant concepts: *human development* defined as a process that enlarges people's choices including freedom, dignity, self-respect and social status; *human poverty* meaning deprivation of essential capabilities such as a long and healthy life, knowledge, economic resources and community participation.

**Poverty is perceived in various ways...**

Many-stranded concepts of poverty reflect the reality of the poor. But they make the tasks of identifying the poor and of monitoring progress more complicated. Some dimensions lack good measures, and one strand may be inconsistent with others. Furthermore, there may be a risk that policies and activities merely get poverty labels with no real changes towards more effective pro-poor policy action.

The *Guidelines* address both of these concerns and present a practical and conceptually adequate definition of poverty, placing it in a broader framework of causes and appropriate policy actions. Identifying causal links and assessing the likely effectiveness of different policy instruments is necessary for achieving poverty reduction.

### Defining poverty: the core dimensions

*... relating to different kinds of personal and household capabilities...*

An adequate concept of poverty should include all the most important areas in which people of either gender are deprived and perceived as incapacitated in different societies and local contexts. It should encompass the causal links between the core dimensions of poverty and the central importance of gender and environmentally sustainable development (Figure 1).

**Economic capabilities** mean the ability to earn an income, to consume and to have assets, which are all key to food security, material well-being and social status. These aspects are often raised by poor people, along with secure access to productive financial and physical resources: land, implements and animals, forests and fishing waters, credit and decent employment.

**Human capabilities** are based on health, education, nutrition, clean water and shelter. These are core elements of well-being as well as crucial means to improving livelihoods. Disease and illiteracy are barriers to productive work, and thus to economic and other capabilities for poverty reduction. Reading and writing facilitate communication with others, which is crucial in social and political participation. Education, especially for girls, is considered the single most effective means for defeating poverty and some of its major causal factors, for example illness – in particular AIDS – and excessive fertility.

**Political capabilities** include human rights, a voice and some influence over public policies and political priorities. Deprivation of basic political freedoms or human rights is a major aspect of poverty. This includes arbitrary, unjust and even violent action by the police or other public authorities that is a serious concern of poor people. Powerlessness aggravates other dimensions of poverty. The politically weak have neither the voice in policy reforms nor secure access to resources required to rise out of poverty.

**Socio-cultural capabilities** concern the ability to participate as a valued member of a community. They refer to social status, dignity and other cultural conditions for belonging to a society which are highly valued by the poor themselves. Participatory poverty assessments indicate that geographic and social isolation is the *main* meaning of poverty for people in many local societies; other dimensions are seen as contributing factors.

**Protective capabilities** enable people to withstand economic and external shocks. Thus, they are important for preventing poverty. Insecurity and vulnerability are crucial dimensions of poverty with strong links to all other dimensions. Poor people indicate that hunger and food insecurity are core concerns along with other risks like illness, crime, war and destitution. To a large extent, poverty is experienced intermittently in response to seasonal variations and external shocks – natural disasters, economic crises and violent conflicts. Dynamic concepts are needed because people move in and out of poverty. Today's poor are only partly the same people as yesterday's or tomorrow's. Some are chronically poor or inherit their poverty; others are in temporary or transient poverty.

## Figure 1. Interactive dimensions of poverty and well-being

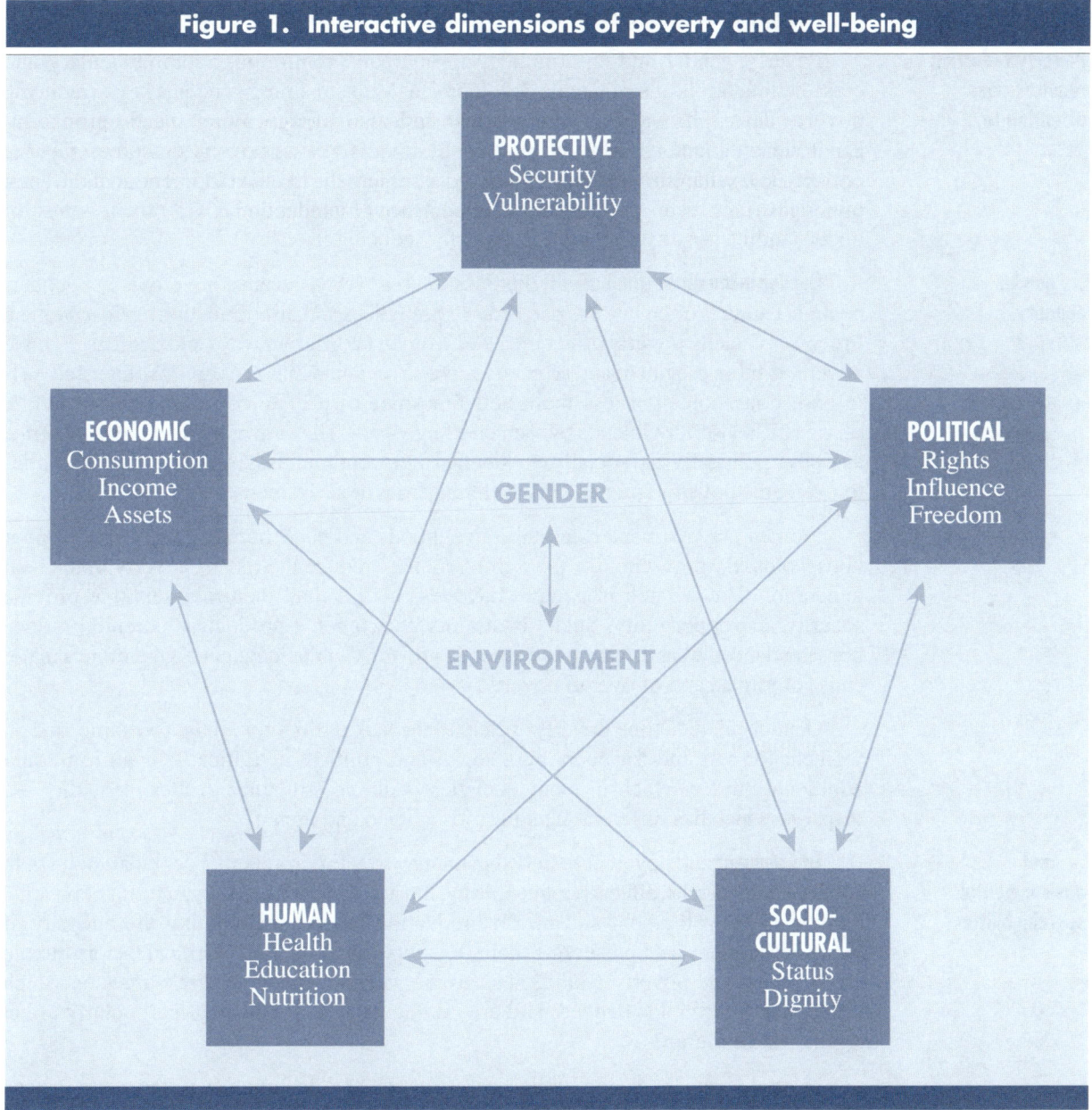

The links indicated by arrows in Figure 1 are significant. Each box represents an important dimension of poverty, which affects – and is affected by – all the others. Household members may consume little and be vulnerable partly because they lack assets, often because of inadequate income, poor health and education, or because they lose their few productive assets as a result of shocks. Lack of human rights and political freedoms indicates a risk of violent conflict shocks. Vulnerability and social exclusion hamper human and political capabilities, reducing incomes and assets, and so on. The fact that different dimensions of poverty are tightly interrelated, while still distinct and imperfectly correlated, is a major reason for a multidimensional concept.

**... that are interrelated...**

**... yet useful to distinguish for analysis and policy action.**

## Poverty links with gender and environment

**Poverty reduction requires close attention to...**

Poverty, gender and environment are mutually reinforcing, complementary and cross-cutting facets of sustainable development. Mainstreaming gender is key to reducing poverty across its various dimensions, and also to improving the environment. Environmental factors influence gender relations as well as poverty outcomes. Gender equality and environmental sustainability are international development goals in their own right. This section addresses the importance of gender and environment issues for understanding poverty and as conditions for reducing it.

**... gender equality...**

**Gender inequality** concerns all dimensions of poverty, because poverty is not gender-neutral.[3] Cultures often involve deep-rooted prejudices and discrimination against women. Processes causing poverty affect men and women in different ways and degrees. Female poverty is more prevalent and typically more severe than male poverty. Women and girls in poor households get less than their fair share of private consumption and public services. They suffer violence by men on a large scale. They are more likely to be illiterate as well as politically and socially excluded in their communities. Hence, women's abilities to overcome poverty are generally different from those of men.

Women play a crucial role in the livelihoods and basic human capabilities of poor households. By providing for their children, they reduce the risk of poverty in the next generation. But women in general have less access than men to assets that provide security and opportunity. Such constraints on women's productive potential reduce household incomes and aggregate economic growth. Gender inequality is therefore a major cause of female and of overall poverty.

Gender-related "time poverty" refers to the lack of time for all the tasks imposed on women, for rest and for economic, social and political activities. It is an important additional burden which in many societies is due to structural gender inequality – a disparity which has different meanings for women and men.

**... and environmental sustainability.**

**Environment** and poverty are linked in many ways. Environmental degradation, in both rural and urban areas, affects poor people the most. Conversely, it is also a result of poverty. Sustainable development and poverty reduction require maintaining the integrity of natural ecosystems and preserving their life-supporting functions.[4] Critical factors linking environment and poverty include security of access to the natural resources on which many poor households depend, and environmental health risks that particularly affect women and children.

In rural areas, land degradation, deforestation and declining fish stocks are serious threats to the livelihood and health of poor people, along with pollution of water and indoor air. Yet, the rural poor often lack alternatives to unsustainable use of fragile land for subsistence agriculture, livestock ranging and woodcutting, thus aggravating soil loss. The increasing scarcity of good land and clean water can fuel social and political instability and local, national and regional conflict, unless the competing needs of different users can be peacefully and equitably reconciled.

Poor people in both rural and urban areas are highly vulnerable to devastating natural disasters[5] such as droughts, floods, typhoons/hurricanes and rising sea levels that threaten entire populations in small islands and low-lying coastal areas, especially in poor countries. The incidence and severity of these may be aggravated by global climate change, which is expected to accelerate. Economic growth in developing countries – while important for poverty reduction – generates increased emissions of greenhouse gases that affect global climate change.

The urban poor often live in overcrowded and unsanitary conditions near contaminated areas, industrial sites and heavy road traffic. High-density and poor informal urban settlements are vulnerable to such calamities as landslides and fire. And in both rural and urban dwellings, indoor smoke pollution causes serious health problems. Other environmental risks concern safety at work, for example agricultural workers' exposure to pesticides and other hazardous chemicals.[6]

## Who are the poor?

This question is relevant for different levels of society: individual, household, community, district, regional, and so on. National demographic and household surveys provide useful data on average levels of income or consumption and their distribution, but without more specific information, the poor cannot be identified through national statistics. Pro-poor planning should define social categories using such attributes as gender, ethnicity, religion and culture, location and livelihood status as well as the type of household: that is, the number of members, their age distribution and the gender of its head.

**There are several sources of data on poverty...**

In drawing poverty profiles, poverty assessments at country level use data mainly from household surveys and, also, from national indicators of human development. Participatory poverty assessments (PPAs) provide multidimensional profiles with both quantitative data and qualitative information. Although, in some cases, PPAs are most suitable for designing policies and interventions, they are also expensive.

The dimensions and measures of poverty may be inconsistent, which complicates the task of identifying the poor. For example, people may be income-poor even if their children, including girls, are enrolled in primary school and the national child and maternal mortality rates have been reduced in line with the MDGs, and illiterate people can earn more than "US$1" per day, etc. The more information available about such differences and trade-offs, the more suitable the design of policies and actions can be.

**... but more and better information is needed.**

Despite the difficulty of precise measurement, knowledge from different sources can often be used to identify the poor. Social categories known for severe poverty in several dimensions are indigenous, minority and socially excluded groups, refugees or displaced persons, the mentally or physically disabled and HIV/AIDS victims. Women and children are especially vulnerable, for example elderly widows and unsupported female- and child-headed households, and street children. In many societies, these groups are the poorest of the poor and require special attention in policy action for poverty reduction.

## How can poverty be measured and monitored?

The next issue is how to measure the diverse dimensions of poverty. Measurement is necessary for monitoring the degree to which policy goals have been met, for assessing the impact of particular policies and programmes, and for identifying the poor. Best practice is to collect data that differentiate according to gender, age and other social categories.[7] The adequacy of various tools for measuring poverty depends on the availability of data and the purpose of measurement. The less tangible dimensions of poverty are more costly and time-consuming to measure and to quantify.

**Poverty can be measured in various ways...**

Composite indexes that include both economic and other poverty dimensions may provide more solid comparable quantitative measures than measures in one dimension only. The most prominent ones have been developed by UNDP in the annual Human Development Report (HDR).[8] They have been vital in drawing attention to the multidimensional and serious problems of poverty. But to some extent, the choice of

**... that are useful for different purposes...**

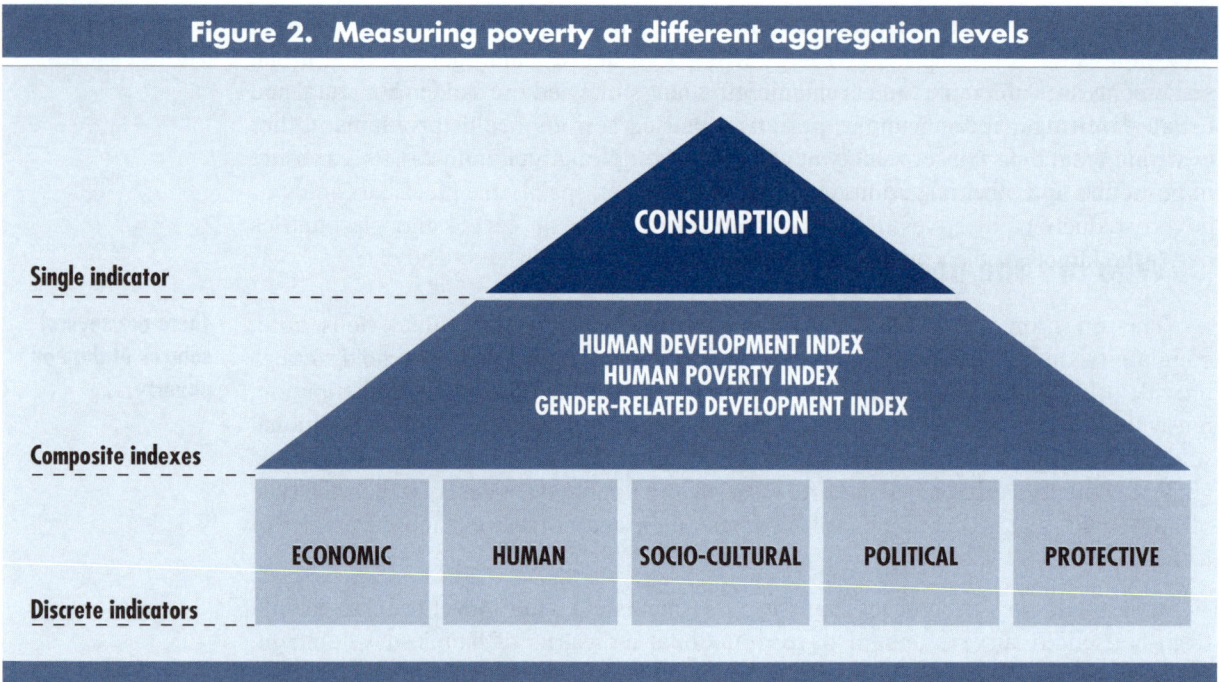

**Figure 2. Measuring poverty at different aggregation levels**

Single indicator

CONSUMPTION

Composite indexes

HUMAN DEVELOPMENT INDEX
HUMAN POVERTY INDEX
GENDER-RELATED DEVELOPMENT INDEX

Discrete indicators

| ECONOMIC | HUMAN | SOCIO-CULTURAL | POLITICAL | PROTECTIVE |

indicators and the weights assigned to them is arbitrary, and trade-offs between them are not captured. Thus, discrete poverty measures are still more useful for specific planning purposes.

**... such as specific poverty action...**

Different kinds of measures have their uses: relative, contextual, qualitative, and multidimensional indicators are best for understanding a specific situation and intervening in it effectively. But they are less useful for comparisons or for overall poverty monitoring and impact assessments, which require absolute, simple and quantified measures (Figure 2).

The top of Figure 2 illustrates the simple consumption or income expenditure measure available from household surveys in a large number of countries. This is useful for comparative analyses of poverty over time in a country and among different countries, and for overall poverty monitoring. In other words, at the top there is a bird's eye view measure of poverty. The middle section represents composite indexes.

The bottom section portrays the foundation for measuring poverty in its various dimensions. It is closer to the local community level and so is of more use in detailed planning and monitoring. National data on human development are routinely collected in surveys and presented in global tables in HDR and the World Development Reports (WDR) from the World Bank. For the remaining dimensions there are no good methods to standardise and quantify measures that would permit comparisons. But several countries have undertaken participatory poverty assessments that provide very useful qualitative and multidimensional information about poverty.

**... or general poverty comparisons...**

The narrow approach to measuring poverty permits the identification and statistical analysis of those households falling under an absolute poverty line, which is set at a minimum standard of nutrition and consumption. This is necessary for monitoring the numbers as well as the proportion of poor people over time and among countries,[9] and the depth and severity of poverty. The most common poverty lines for international comparisons are US$1 a day for low-income countries, US$2 for middle-income countries, and US$4 for transition economies. Many countries have their own poverty lines reflecting different social, economic and climatic conditions in determining what is considered an acceptable minimum income.

Having considered the meaning of poverty and how poverty can be measured, the next step in formulating a poverty strategy is to specify indicators and goals. Governments must set poverty reduction targets and identify means of assessing and monitoring them. Goals and benchmark indicators should be specified according to data sources that are available for the period for which they are set. They should conform to the economic, political and socio-cultural realities of each country and specify the precise meaning of poverty reduction objectives. The goals should be related to the MDGs, though countries may have targets of their own for different indicators or for different end dates.

**... or setting goals and benchmarks.**

It is vital to disaggregate national indicators into others which will distinguish outcomes for different categories of people: for example by gender, age and other social categories, geographic or administrative region, and by rural and urban areas. Tracking inequalities in this way provides early warnings on important poverty factors including conflict risk. Popular participation in the process of setting goals and indicators can generate national consensus on poverty reduction. Good data are essential for analysing outcomes against which governments can be held accountable, and for monitoring how diverse groups of poor people fare.

## Why does poverty persist?

There are two further steps in formulating poverty strategies: identifying and ranking the *causes* of each dimension of poverty in a given area or country, and designing *policies and actions* to address these causes. This section addresses the first step.

Among the root causes of poverty, some are linked to immutable factors like climate, geography and history. By contrast, deficient governance, which is subject to change, includes a core set of factors that perpetuate poverty. Entrenched corruption and rent-seeking élites, lack of respect for human rights, weak institutions and inefficient bureaucracies, lack of social cohesion and political will to undertake reforms are all common features of bad governance and inimical to sustainable development and poverty reduction. In extreme but alas not rare cases, failures of governance lead to violent conflict and the collapse of states. Inequality by gender or other social and economic categories is another major factor perpetuating poverty, as well as environmental degradation and rapid population growth. An emerging and absolutely critical poverty issue is HIV/AIDS, which particularly affects young women and children, many of whom are orphaned.

**The common causes of poverty are well-known...**

These factors can all lead to inadequate economic growth, which is a major cause of poverty. Others include governance and equity defects, economic policy and market failures, capital flight, low savings and investments, and distorted incentives, all of which lower productivity and incomes. High inflation is a particularly harmful tax on the real incomes and savings of the poor. Crumbling physical and social infrastructure both follows from and aggravates economic stagnation and decline. Protectionism in potential export markets as well as volatility and falling trends in the terms-of-trade are international economic causes of poverty. Debt overhang, both domestic and international, is another key catalyst.

Ranking the most important causal poverty factors in any given country is far more complex than identifying key social groups among the poor, or recording the available descriptive poverty profiles. For these reasons ranking is rarely attempted, but it is, nonetheless, essential for effective poverty reduction. All national poverty reduction policies and agency strategies should include an attempt at categorising and assessing causes. Strategic planning calls for decisions, choices and priorities, and ranking policy instruments by likely impact is the hallmark of a robust approach.

**... but it is essential to identify and rank the specific causes in each country.**

Formulating a poverty strategy involves a great deal of uncertainty. Managers, agency staff and professional advisers must ensure that their judgements are at least *educated* guesses – that is, fully informed by the data and analyses that are available or that could easily be commissioned at country level.[10]

## Which policy actions are required?

Strategies for poverty reduction and sustainable development should converge and serve as the common platform for programmes and projects in development co-operation. Sustainable development has many aspects: they are economic, social, environmental and institutional and call for comprehensive approaches, many of which cut across sectors and institutional boundaries. Any strategy for the effective and sustainable reduction of poverty has to include the following policy elements, which are complementary and not in order of priority:[11]

**Comprehensive approaches are needed, including...**

a)   *Pro-poor economic growth: pace and quality.*

b)   *Empowerment, rights and pro-poor governance.*

c)   *Basic social services for human development.*

d)   *Human security: reducing vulnerability and managing shocks.*

e)   *Mainstreaming gender and enhancing gender equality.*

f)   *Mainstreaming environmental sustainability using sustainable livelihood approaches.*

### Pro-poor economic growth: pace and quality

Economic growth is crucial in reducing poverty and both its pace and quality matter – its composition, distribution and sustainability are particularly vital. The lack of economic resources is a key dimension of poverty as well as a major cause of its other dimensions. Equitable growth in the national income also reduces income poverty in most households and, on the other hand, effective strategies for sustained poverty reduction engender income growth in most households and in the aggregate GDP.

**... economic reform policies for pro-poor growth,...**

A national economy can grow in different ways that can reduce poverty, promote gender equality and sustain viable development to greater or lesser degrees.[12] The general links between economic growth and poverty reduction are significant; both the average incidence and the depth of poverty tend to fall with growth.[13] Economic growth can create opportunities for poor people, but poverty will decline only if the conditions are in place for them to take advantage of those opportunities.

Effective pro-poor growth strategies and policies differ between countries depending on resource endowments, levels of technology and human capital, and the historical, institutional and socio-cultural context. In general, a competitive market economy favours private sector productivity, savings and investments that engender economic growth, under the following key conditions:

■ A framework of policy, administrative, legal and financial institutions conducive to good public sector and corporate governance, and sustainable development.

■ Macroeconomic and political stability.

■ Adequate and accessible physical and social service infrastructure for all population groups.

- Secure access for poor women and men to resources such as land, finance and human capabilities.

- Labour-intensive forms of production.

- Social policies fostering cohesion, mobility, protection, redistribution and gender equality.

A good legal and institutional governance framework is essential for enhancing the opportunities for poor women and men to climb out of poverty. Requirements include corporate governance systems that produce a sound environment for private investment, and a regulatory environment that engenders both competition and systemic stability, with particular attention to the financial sector. Structural reforms of policies, incentives and institutions are often required in such areas as fiscal management, trade, labour market, financial sector, infrastructure and land use.

**... enhancing governance and institutions,...**

Macroeconomic stability with low inflation and limited volatility in prices and production, efficient competitive markets, and adequate policies promoting savings and investments – private and public – are all key elements. Public policy should proactively facilitate an enabling environment for private sector investment and growth, which is crucial for creating employment. There should be a considered balance and partnership among the three main spheres of society: government, business and civil society.

Achieving pro-poor growth requires policies and programmes that enable poor people to use their assets and capabilities to generate enhanced and sustainable livelihoods, for example through micro-finance programmes or through the promotion of labour-intensive production of goods and services. Governments need to tackle the inequalities of opportunity that face poor people by improving access to basic social services, particularly education and health, which are essential human capital investments for broadly-based growth. And fiscal policies – both expenditures and revenues – should be designed to promote poverty reduction.

**...reducing inflation and stimulating the private sector,...**

For small, poor economies, the global economy offers great potential for reducing poverty. But these countries are also at greatest risk of economic disruption from increased openness – for example from sudden reversals in short-term capital flows or from shocks in the terms-of-trade. Hence integration requires prudent management to ensure that the poor benefit from trade-led growth. This involves building capacity and exploring opportunities for trade while taking policy action to mitigate the increased risks of globalisation, for example from capital outflows, environmental degradation, unemployment or the undermining of core labour standards. Regional integration can be appropriate as an intermediate step towards trade liberalisation, permitting the weak economies to adapt gradually to larger, more competitive markets.

**... developing trade capacity,...**

Both asset and income inequality – by gender or other categories (ethnic, social, regional, etc.) – are a major impediment to poverty reduction. Such inequalities give a double, and negative impetus to poverty by lowering both the pace and the poverty impact of GDP growth. Sharp and rising inequalities reduce the voice of the poor in policy and increase the risks of conflict and violence. Public policies aimed at reducing inequalities are important, but require the tactful building of political coalitions to overcome vested interests. Development agencies can facilitate reforms through policy dialogue as well as through financial and technical support for such pro-poor structural change as land reform.[14]

Faster growth will improve the prospects for reducing poverty in both high- and low-inequality countries, but to reduce income poverty by half, high-inequality countries will, on average, need to grow twice as fast as low-inequality countries. This is not feasible, and thus more equitable growth is a necessary condition for achieving the international development goal for income poverty reduction.[15]

**... reducing inequalities and improving poor people's access to assets and social services, especially in rural areas,...**

Most poor people in developing countries still live in rural areas. They tend to be more deprived of access to health, education, food and markets than urban households and this gap is not shrinking. The proportion of urban poverty is increasing rapidly.[16] Rural poverty and the greater opportunities in urban areas incite poor people to migrate, increasing urban unemployment and poverty. Hence, pro-poor rural (on- and off-farm) development is a key priority for the overall reduction of poverty.

Rural and urban poverty needs to be tackled with complementary policies. Rural and urban areas are linked through kinship, migration, trade and remittances and such links are important for stimulating pro-poor economic growth. Moreover, urban agriculture provides livelihoods for a considerable number of the urban poor. Sustainable and gender-balanced growth in small-scale agriculture and rural services is particularly effective for reducing poverty in both rural and urban areas. It creates strong backward and forward linkages through increased demand and supply, stimulating growth in income and employment.

The rural poor need enhanced access to resources in important but somewhat neglected areas: physical and financial assets, technology and natural resources (land and water), markets and institutions.[17] Support for research into and the extension of improved seeds, micro-irrigation, micro-finance and public works are all examples of important tools for helping poor rural women and men rise out of poverty.

**... while also responding to the challenge of urban poverty reduction.**

Urban poverty is complex and challenging. Land use planning for sustainable urban development is crucial. The rapidly growing cities of developing countries, especially in Africa and Latin America, cause huge environmental problems and foster social and physical insecurity while lacking traditional social support systems. This calls for providing social services and public utilities of good quality, and for special programmes aiming to raise the productivity of poor women and men. At the same time, it is important to avoid distorting subsidies that could lead to a bigger influx of poor rural people and a consequent worsening of urban poverty. Market development through institutional reform and improved infrastructure is crucial. Land tenure is important, as in rural areas, for security and for the necessary collateral for starting small businesses. The informal sector plays an important role in containing urban poverty, but there is a need for increased attention to minimum labour and environmental standards.

### Empowerment, rights and pro-poor governance

Poverty often means powerlessness, injustice and exclusion from social participation as a result of discrimination and, more generally, a lack of human - including political - rights. Empowering poor women and men requires democratic governance with popular participation in policy-making, programme design and implementation, a civil society with representative community organisations, human rights and the rule of law. Independent media can play an important role in developing a culture of democracy.

**Pro-poor governance is a crucial element,...**

Empowerment is about enhancing the capacity of poor women and men to influence political and social processes that affect their lives. Depending on prevailing conditions, poor people can exercise their human rights and mobilise to empower themselves. The process of democratisation empowers women and men to demand their rights, but in too many cases, the powerful and privileged entrench their positions, usurping political institutions for selfish benefit.[18]

Rights-based approaches to poverty reduction are increasingly in focus, linking empowerment of poor women and men and the rights of children to the framework of norms, standards and principles of the international agreements on human rights.[19] They address the causes of poverty by identifying rights-holders and duty-bearers for the realisation of all human rights – civil, cultural, political, social and economic. The emphasis on human rights shows that justice is a matter of rights, not charity. Recognising this, and being aware of how to claim rights may increase confidence among poor and socially excluded groups and facilitate greater participation in development.

**... based on democratic empowerment and human – including political – rights,...**

A rights-based approach involves strengthening the ability of courts and other institutions to promote and protect the universal rights of women and men, including the rights to adequate information, to decent work and to organise unions. A democratic political process and effective economic, legal and judiciary systems are important for improving the framework conditions for empowering poor and socially excluded groups. This includes effective and transparent institutions of governance, democratic accountability and a free press. Efforts to improve governance and reduce corruption by strengthening accountability and service orientation in the public sector are crucial. They need to be buttressed by civil service reforms to ensure an adequate incentive structure facing public sector staff, including decent and regularly paid wages.

**... controlling corruption and increasing accountability,...**

Political devolution and increased participation by poor women and men in local or regional government promote empowerment and pro-poor outcomes. A related reform is administrative decentralisation, which has the potential to reduce major corruption and improve the efficiency of public service delivery. But decentralisation in highly inegalitarian societies, with weak social organisation among poor groups, may serve mainly to aggravate misrule by unchecked local élites. To ensure a pro-poor impact of decentralisation, local governance and democratic accountability must be strengthened.

**... which may be enhanced by democratic decentralisation.**

### Basic social services for human development

Human development is the process of expanding human capabilities and choices – what people do and can do in their lives. Human development includes the expansion of income and wealth as well as adequate nutrition, safe water, good and affordable medical services, schools and transportation, decent shelter and employment, and secure livelihoods. Sustained pro-poor economic growth raises the income and consumption of poor women and men and it also provides resources for social sector services. Wide access to quality social services engenders economic growth by increasing people's productive capabilities.

**Quality social services are indispensable for human development and promoting pro-poor growth...**

HIV/AIDS and other increasingly prevalent poverty-related diseases like malaria and tuberculosis imperil social cohesion, economic growth – and poverty reduction. AIDS has become an absolutely critical development issue in Africa and this may soon be so in Asia, with its much larger population. High-level political recognition of the central importance of this issue and the related areas of sexual and reproductive health and rights is necessary for any successful human development and poverty reduction strategy.

To live long, healthy and gratifying lives requires access to public social services of good quality that provide preventive and curative health care and formal or informal schooling. Basic education – for girls, boys, women and men – is the single most important factor in human development, in poverty reduction, in containing AIDS and in reducing fertility rates. Poor women and men are often deprived of access to adequate social services because insufficient public resources are allocated and governance is weak. Special measures can encourage outreach and better access to basic services for poor women, men and children. Pro-poor methods of financing public social services with taxes, and in some cases user fees, should be carefully studied, designed and monitored to ensure access, affordability and quality.

**... but only if public funds are used efficiently for improving service delivery to the poor.**

The proportion of public spending allocated to primary education and health in poor countries is often used as an indicator of the poverty orientation of government policies.[20] While public spending is important, increased resources will only help if used efficiently. It is crucial to improve the allocation of social sector spending in the context of broad sector policies and strategies that address trade-offs: for example between basic and higher education, and between primary and curative health care. Improving governance for human development is an important area for policy action.

## Human security: reducing vulnerability and managing shocks

**Insecurity is both a dimension and a cause of poverty...**

Human security means safeguarding human development by protecting people from deprivation as a result of disruptions or shocks. Poor women and men see insecurity as both a major dimension and a principal cause of poverty. The risks facing the poor are substantial and have a variety of sources, including livelihood risks due to food shortages, sickness, old age, natural calamities, and also unemployment and other economic adjustment shocks. These risks call for social protection programmes as a priority area for social policy. Poor women are at particular risk of domestic violence.[21] And poor workers are subject to serious occupational hazards.[22]

**... that includes crime, conflicts and calamities,...**

Overall, the vulnerability of poor people is rising as new sources of violent conflict and crime emerge, and as risks of natural disaster from extreme climatic shocks and seasonal variations increase. Inequality between ethnic and social groups can and sometimes does lead to violent conflicts. These perpetuate and aggravate poverty and lead to a toll of dead, wounded, disabled and displaced people. They further ruin infrastructure, economic performance and social fabric. Conflicts invariably destroy social capital and deepen failures in governance, sometimes to the point of state collapse.[23]

**... high-lighting the need for a human security approach.**

A human security approach identifies and addresses the sources of risk affecting poor women and men. It breaks out of the increasingly artificial separation between conflict prevention and resolution, post-conflict reconstruction, natural disaster preparedness and relief, and work on rights-based governance. An increasingly important approach to anti-poverty action concentrates on reducing the multiple sources of risk (including the environmental risks caused by increasing lack of fertile land, safe water and clean air) and assisting poor people to contend with them.

## Mainstreaming gender and enhancing gender equality

**Durable poverty reduction requires mainstreaming both gender equality,...**

Gender inequality is both a major cause of poverty and a major impediment to sustainable development. Reducing gender inequality means improving women's access to employment, credit and other productive resources, enabling women to earn income. This has been found to contribute to more rapid and pro-poor aggregate economic growth, benefiting women and children as well as men.

Poverty strategies must address the differences between women and men in their access to resources and opportunities. Outcomes are affected by the amount and variety of material and intangible resources available to a household and, not least, by resource distribution within the household. Gender inequality is prevalent not only within poor households but also at the communal and national level.

Mainstreaming gender into policy can be a fruitful subject of dialogue and co-operation among governments, civil society and development agencies. Together these institutions can reduce gender differences in access to basic services, to economic opportunities and to such assets as land and finance, to labour markets, to political participation and to knowledge and technology.

Effective anti-poverty strategies need to consider existing gender relations, paying particular attention to women's time poverty caused by the double burden of paid work and their unpaid care activities. Governments need to recognise gender exclusion when shaping legal, institutional and policy frameworks, for instance in allocations of public expenditure. In several countries, household crop production, children's health and education, and birth rates have all improved as a result of gender-specific national budgets. Careful monitoring and evaluation would give greater insight into the effectiveness of "gender budgets".

### Mainstreaming environmental sustainability using sustainable livelihood approaches

The international development goals, which include income poverty reduction, social development and environmental sustainability and regeneration, are closely linked to the political principle of sustainable development. In this context, a useful policy approach is the sustainable livelihood methodology with its focus on broad-based rural development. Better access to education, health, water, land titles, technology and advisory services, communications and credits are seen as crucial to improving the capability of the rural poor to increase on- and off-farm incomes. Efforts should focus on the diversity of livelihoods and address the systemic conditions that constrain the ability of poor women and men to overcome poverty, for example by increasing farm productivity and food security.

**... and environmental sustainability.**

The concept of livelihood comprises the capabilities[24] and activities required to secure socially adequate living standards. A livelihood is sustainable when it can cope with stresses and shocks without undermining its natural resource base. The means of livelihood available to poor women and men include, but are not restricted to, natural resources. They are affected by economic factors and governance, external shocks and trends as well as by natural endowments. Recognising this provides a basis for action that combines poverty reduction with sustainable development.

This approach recognises the importance of micro-meso-macro links, focusing on the policy and institutional mechanisms that influence the availability and value of the resources on which poor women and men depend for their livelihoods. Interventions must consider all circumstances affecting the livelihoods of groups of poor people, including power and dependency relations, rather than making assumptions based on broad generalisations or sector-specific policy. The sustainable livelihoods approach entails working in bottom-up fashion, starting from the perceptions and priorities expressed by poor people. Their perceptions and needs must then be reconciled with the views of agencies and authorities, which are looking at the sustainability of development on a national and international scale.

## Box 4. Rural poverty–environment–sustainable development policy convergence

The rural poor, and notably the landless, depend on their surrounding ecosystems – forests, wetlands and coastal fisheries – to meet their needs for food, fuel, fodder and medicinal plants. They are therefore directly threatened by resource degradation. Policies to reduce rural poverty will require consistent sustainable development policies concerning agriculture and the environment, including to:

■ Strengthen the rights of the poor to secure access to productive resources and social services.

■ Give priority to investments in sustainable management of ecologically fragile areas.

■ Foster the diffusion of appropriate, high-yielding and sustainable cropping methods.

■ Redirect resources to the poor.

■ Support off-farm rural livelihood diversification.

■ Integrate the poor into decision-making processes.

## Conclusion

Being strategic about poverty reduction means achieving clarity about goals, and then devoting attention to two further issues – identifying the key causal links and choosing the most effective forms of intervention. Poverty is multidimensional and needs to be understood in its different dimensions in the strategic planning of policies, programmes and projects. A quantitative income or composite index may be adequate for purposes of comparison over time and between countries.

Prioritising causes and choosing the most effective policy instruments for anti-poverty action is difficult, but essential. Table 1 may facilitate this task; it invites the user to select and rank poverty determinants and forms of intervention most likely to reach desired outcomes in a particular context – on a global, (sub-)continental, national, regional or community level. Agency staff need access to general guidance based on research and practical experience, and they should be expected to be conversant with the data and analyses available – or which could be made available – at country level.

## Table 1. Tackling the poverty complex:
## An illustration of causal factors, policy action and outcome indicators

This table provides a summary of factors causing poverty, policy actions to deal with these and indicators for monitoring the poverty outcomes. The table should not necessarily be read as a matrix with causality links going horizontally from left to right. Each poverty factor may require policy action in several areas. A policy action may be linked primarily with one set of factors and outcomes but can also affect others. To a considerable extent, causes, actions and outcomes mutually affect each other.

| CAUSAL FACTORS:<br>■ typical factors | POLICY ACTION:<br>■ typical areas and measures | OUTCOMES:<br>■ typical indicators (and sources) |
| --- | --- | --- |
| **Economic structures:**<br>■ pace, patterns and quality of growth<br>■ rates of saving and investments (including sector allocations and choice of technology)<br>■ inflation<br>■ microeconomic incentive structures<br>■ trade (export market access, terms-of-trade trends and volatility, trade policies)<br>■ inequality of access to assets (by gender, class, area)<br>■ unequal access to markets and services<br>■ labour market conditions<br>■ institutional gender bias in labour and other markets<br>■ unsustainable resource use<br><br>**Availability of and access to quality resources:**<br>■ natural capital (water, forests, land, etc.), including common-pool natural resources, which are often overexploited<br>■ physical capital (animals, implements, equipment, infrastructure)<br>■ human capital (health, education, skills)<br>■ social capital (benefits of association)<br>■ financial capital (savings, credit) | **Pro-poor economic growth:**<br>■ good economic governance: predictable, transparent policy-making<br>■ macroeconomic stabilisation policies<br>■ measures to counter urban bias/promote agricultural growth and rural development<br>■ proactive management of external market integration, starting with opening regional markets<br>■ asset creation and redistribution<br>■ measures to increase market access, especially for women, and to remove market distortions<br>■ financial sector development and supervision, including prudent regulation of external flows, and gender-fair access to financial resources<br>■ promote local economic development, including micro-finance and business advice services<br>■ integration of growth policies in the framework of national strategies for sustainable development (nssd)<br><br>**Empowerment, rights and pro-poor governance:**<br>■ rule of law under democratic governance<br>■ legal and advocacy work on human rights<br>■ support for civil society and citizenship rights<br>■ promotion of economic and social rights of/for the poor<br>■ capacity-building to strengthen community confidence and empowerment to access rights<br>■ the right to freedom of association and to decent work<br><br>**Basic social services for human development:**<br>■ prioritised national anti-poverty and gender-sensitive budgets and expenditure management<br>■ pro-poor allocation of resources within the social sectors<br>■ review financing and incidence of taxes and user charges, impact on access and quality<br>■ good governance of social services with incentives to improve services | **Economic capabilities:**<br>■ incidence, depth and severity of household consumption poverty (household surveys)<br>■ asset portfolios of poorest (household surveys)<br>■ consumption shares and time use of men and women (in-depth case studies)<br><br>**Political capabilities:**<br>■ self-assessed powerlessness (participatory poverty assessments)<br>■ survey evidence of local power relations and their dynamics<br>■ surveys of gender balance in decision-making at all levels<br>■ regulations for decentralised decision-making<br><br>**Human capabilities:**<br>■ stunting and wasting<br>■ infant and child mortality<br>■ maternal mortality<br>■ HIV prevalence/AIDS mortality<br>■ community-based disease monitoring indicators<br>■ education<br>■ gender balance in schools<br><br>**Social capabilities:**<br>■ analysis of local rankings of poverty/well-being (participatory poverty assessments)<br>■ evidence of social interaction patterns by gender, ethnicity and other social categories<br>■ number and degree of activity of community-based organisations<br><br>Continued on next page |

## Table 1. Tackling the poverty complex: An illustration of causal factors, policy action and outcome indicators (continued)

| CAUSAL FACTORS:<br>■ typical factors | POLICY ACTION:<br>■ typical areas and measures | OUTCOMES:<br>■ typical indicators (and sources) |
|---|---|---|
| **Governance and public service provision:**<br>■ lack of popular participation and transparency in the political process<br>■ lack of respect for human rights, including freedom of association, expression and media<br>■ corruption<br>■ ineffective delivery of public services<br>■ class, gender and ethnic biases in uptake of services<br>■ limited access and very low quality services for poorest<br>■ centralised decision-making and structures<br><br>**Demographic patterns:**<br>■ high population growth rates (delayed demographic transition, excessive fertility, frequent pregnancies)<br>■ mortality shocks, especially HIV/AIDS<br>■ geographic isolation<br>■ rural-to-urban migration<br><br>**Social exclusion:**<br>■ those excluded experience cumulative limitations to access<br>■ erosion or non-existence of mechanisms to maintain minimal social functioning by poorest (aged, widows, the disabled, indigenous people)<br>■ distance and social bias silences voices of poorest<br>■ economic poverty forces poorest into livelihoods incompatible with social dignity<br>■ patriarchal cultural and legal patterns<br>■ alcoholism<br>■ violence against women<br><br>**Shocks and conflicts:**<br>■ expulsion/displacement of populations owing to war<br>■ intra-state conflict<br>■ natural disasters<br>■ economic shocks<br>■ state collapse/social disintegration | **Mainstreaming gender and enhancing gender equality:**<br>■ legal and educational work on women's rights, including sexual and reproductive health and rights, and domestic violence<br>■ poverty and gender-sensitive outreach services in agriculture, education and health<br>■ support for advocacy on time poverty<br><br>**Mainstreaming environmental sustainability using sustainable livelihood approaches:**<br>■ bottom-up policy design, based on analysis of the context in which rural people live, including the impact of external trends and shocks and seasonal variations, and the coping strategies they adopt<br>■ reforming policies, institutions and organisations that shape the livelihoods of the rural poor<br>■ improve access of the rural poor to physical, human, financial, natural and social assets<br>■ farmer-based research and extension with a focus on food security<br>■ good governance of commons and local services<br>■ active monitoring and protection of natural resources in the context of the national strategy for sustainable development (nssd)<br><br>**Human security: reducing vulnerability and managing shocks:**<br>■ support for peace-building and reconstruction<br>■ support for state security sector reforms under democratic governance<br>■ promoting social coherence through civil society development and multicultural tolerance<br>■ building assets that provide security against disasters and economic shocks, including infrastructure and insurance<br>■ safeguarding functioning social protection systems<br>■ community-level work to identify socially excluded people | **Protective capabilities: security, reduced vulnerability:**<br>■ frequency and impact of conflicts and natural disasters<br>■ population movements<br>■ self-assessed well-being (participatory poverty assessments)<br>■ social surveys, sentinel site reports, "social weather stations" |

# Notes

1. The concepts of poverty and well-being are used as antonyms, at the opposite ends of the range of human conditions. Both concepts are used in the text, depending on the context.

2. Examples of absolute poverty measures are in the Millenium Development Goals (see page 19).

3. See *DAC Guidelines for Gender Equality and Women's Empowerment in Development Co-operation* (1998) and *DAC Source Book on Concepts and Approaches Linked to Gender Equality* (1998).

4. These include the regulation of hydrological cycles, the production of biomass, the assimilation of wastes and many others. They underpin the sustainability of livelihoods through a wide range of economic activities. Beyond critical thresholds, ecosystem degradation becomes irreversible.

5. The distinction between "natural" and "human-made" disasters is not absolutely clear. See *Guidelines for Aid Agencies on Disaster Mitigation*, *DAC Guidelines on Aid and Environment No. 7* (1994).

6. See footnote 30.

7. UNDP statistics are to a large extent gender-differentiated and therefore useful as broad indicators of the degree of gender discrimination and inequality.

8. The Human Development Index (HDI), the Gender-related Development Index (GDI), the Gender Empowerment Measure (GEM), the Human Poverty Index (HPI-1 for developing countries and HPI-2 for OECD and transition countries). HDR also provides multidimensional and gender-differentiated human development indicators.

9. The distinction is important: the MDG for eradicating extreme poverty and hunger refers to the proportion of people under the US$1 a day income poverty line, which has declined over the last decade. However, the number of people under this poverty line has gone up and down, and was about the same in 1998 as in 1987.

10. Further guidance to agencies on country programme management, and on institutional learning and change, is provided in Parts 2 and 5.

11. These priority areas and approaches for strategic policy action correspond broadly but not exactly to the dimensions of poverty and the cross-cutting aspects (gender and environment) identified above. The dimensions of poverty do not correspond exactly to the institutionalised policy areas and strategic approaches that affect them. The socio-cultural dimension and the sustainable livelihoods approach are closely linked but distinct entities.

12. The conversion rate of economic growth into income poverty reduction varies considerably across countries and regions because of different degrees of inequality in literacy, land holdings and other assets. For instance, between 1960 and 1994 the poverty reduction impact varied by a factor of four to five times per percentage point of economic growth per capita between different states in India, and similar differences have been found comparing East Asia and Latin America. (*The Quality of Growth*, World Bank, 2000.)

13. Econometric studies by the World Bank find that while growth in mean income is the most important factor for poverty reduction, it explains slightly less than half of the growth of incomes of the poor. The growth-poverty correlation is significant but partial; income inequality is a major factor, although it does not vary systematically with growth; behind the statistical averages, the experience is diverse. (David Dollar and Aart Kraay: *Growth IS Good for the Poor*, World Bank, 2000; Martin Ravallion: *Growth, Inequality and Poverty: Looking Beyond Averages*, World Bank, 2000.)

14. The poverty incidence in Bangladesh is over 60% in areas where median landholdings are less than 1 acre/household, but only 10% where they are 10 acres.

15. Lucia Hanmer, John Healey, Felix Naschold: *Will Growth Halve Global Poverty by 2015?* ODI Poverty Briefing, 8 July 2000.

16. This is partly a result of statistical and administrative classification. The urban-rural distinction is not clear and national definitions vary considerably.

17. See *The Challenge of Ending Rural Poverty*, International Fund for Agricultural Development (IFAD) Rural Poverty Report 2001.

18. Richard Sandbrook: *Citizenship, Rights and Poverty – Narrowing the Gap between Theory and Practice*. Paper presented to the International Institute for Democracy and Electoral Assistance (IDEA), Democracy Forum 2000.

19. Primarily the UN Universal Declaration of Human Rights (1948); the two International Covenants on *i)* Civil and Political Rights (1966), *ii)* Economic, Social and Cultural Rights (1966); the Conventions on the Elimination of all forms of Racial Discrimination (1966), of Discrimination against Women (1979), of Torture and other Cruel, Inhuman or Degrading Treatment or Punishment (1984), on the Rights of the Child (1989); and the ILO Declaration on Fundamental Principles and Rights at Work (1998).

20. For example, the 20:20 Initiative agreed at the UN Social Summit in Copenhagen 1995 and reconfirmed at the UN Special General Assembly in Geneva 2000, in which development agencies and partner governments undertake to allocate at least this percentage of bilateral official development assistance (ODA) and national budgets, respectively, for basic social services.

21. WHO and UNIFEM report that at least 20% of women in the world have been physically or sexually assaulted. In developing countries, the numbers are much higher — in some countries two-thirds of all rural women and over half in urban areas. World Bank has estimated that worldwide violence against women was as serious a cause of death and incapacity among women of reproductive age as cancer, and a greater cause of ill health than traffic accidents and malaria combined.

22. ILO estimates that workers suffer 250 million occupational accidents and 160 million occupational diseases each year. Deaths and injuries take a particularly heavy toll in developing countries, where large numbers of workers are concentrated in primary and extractive activities such as agriculture, logging, fishing and mining – some of the world's most hazardous industries.

23. See *Conflict, Peace and Development Co-operation on the Threshold of the 21st Century*. Development Co-operation Guidelines Series, OECD/DAC, 1998, and its supplement, *Helping Prevent Violent Conflict: Orientations for External Actors,* OECD/DAC, 2001.

24. Economic, human, political, socio-cultural and protective. See above *Defining poverty: the core dimensions*.

# 2 Forging partnerships for reducing poverty

## Introduction

Achieving results in reducing poverty often pivots on what is done, and how, at the country level. Development agencies have historically had problems "operationalising" agency policies for poverty reduction. Part 2 will show how development agencies can best co-operate with developing countries to build strong partnerships and translate policy into more effective programming and operations in the field.

*Successful efforts to reduce poverty often depend on what is done, and how, at the country level.*

The text begins by setting out the basic principles underpinning an agenda for change geared to improving agencies' performance as partners in the fight against poverty. The scope then narrows to focus on good practice in building partnerships, dealing with diverse partner countries and interacting effectively with other partners. The conclusion summarises priority areas for follow-up actions by agencies in implementing poverty reduction partnerships on the ground.

## Fundamental principles governing poverty reduction partnerships

The basic underlying principles that should govern agency work with partners to reduce poverty are spelled out below.

*Basic principles underpinning agency poverty reduction efforts now include a focus on developing partnerships that promote ownership,...*

**National, regional and local ownership of development strategies, policies and priorities is essential.** Policies and programmes addressing poverty are political because they seek to create opportunities for, and distribute resources to, particular groups in society. Progress will not be achieved unless key national and local stakeholders are committed to the necessary economic and political reforms. Accordingly, widespread ownership of pro-poor policies and programmes by partner stakeholders at national, regional and local levels is of prime importance. At the same time, the quality of governance – in particular government efforts to orient strategies in a pro-poor direction – will continue to be a key consideration for agency support.

**Partnership approaches are crucial for facilitating local ownership.** Successful development partnerships are characterised by certain requirements and modalities that might challenge long-standing practices of some development agencies (see overleaf). Partnerships based on a clear understanding of the rights and responsibilities of each partner and on agreement on objectives and ways of achieving them have proved most successful. Local processes to develop poverty reduction strategies hold promise for becoming key frameworks for building strong country-level working partnerships for tackling poverty (Part 3).

**A sound assessment of the local context is key.** A locally-owned poverty reduction strategy may differ from what agencies consider the best policy package in terms of scope, priorities and timeframe. Agency support for partner country approaches should be based on an assessment of the merits, drawbacks and trade-offs associated with the chosen approach, taking into account the available room for manoeuvre given the prevailing local economic, political and social context.

*... on evaluating the appropriateness of local strategies and promoting strong local participation and gender concerns,...*

### Box 5. Good practice approaches for supporting poverty reduction partnerships

Working in partnership calls for fundamental changes in the ways that development agencies interact with other partners (government, civil society) and with each other (multilateral institutions, other bilateral agencies). It also calls for important changes in the way they work at the country level. The following suggests practical ways of working in partnership.

■ Use the partner country's poverty reduction strategy and the national budget as the general framework for development co-operation.

■ Be sensitive to government leadership.

■ Clarify the roles and responsibilities of the different partners (government, bilateral agencies, international and regional financial institutions, United Nations agencies, civil society, labour, private sector).

■ Never work alone. Before undertaking discussions or actions, search out other partners (from the development assistance community, from government and from civil society) who could participate.

■ Invest in mechanisms for co-ordination (which should be country-led and used for co-ordinating *ex ante* strategic planning and joint implementation), including working out the details of how, when and where to interact with other external and local partners.

■ Promote and consolidate joint work (data collection, analyses, missions, evaluation, management and accountability of aid flows) and share information (data, analysis, policy and programming intentions) with other partners.

■ Simplify and rationalise, where feasible, development agency administrative and financial requirements (for example financial management and accountability, preparatory phases of the project cycle, and reporting and monitoring) and strengthen related partner government systems.

■ Facilitate local mobilisation, participation, monitoring and assessment.

■ Provide capacity-building to strengthen government leadership of poverty reduction co-ordination and consultative processes, and to enable civil society, including women's organisations and gender equality advocates, to engage effectively in the consultation process and to actively monitor and evaluate poverty reduction policies and programmes – while at the same time not undermining partner government authority or national democratic institutions.

**Participation and empowerment must be emphasised.** Participation at all levels and at all stages in development co-operation is a basic precondition for better pro-poor policies, greater accountability in implementation, and more sustainable outcomes through local ownership. Empowering individuals, families and communities is essential for developing human capital and for enabling poor people to merge with the social, political and economic mainstream of their countries and to shape their destinies. Empowering the poor is increasingly recognised as crucial to achieving results in the fight against poverty.

**... on forging long-term relationships...**

**Gender is a key vector for reducing poverty.** Experience and empirical fact have demonstrated the immense impact of activities supporting women's rights, opportunities and empowerment on reducing poverty. Accordingly, *all poverty-focused development co-operation must take gender into account.* Gender-aware development co-operation has direct results in improved livelihoods and reduced discrimination, and is particularly important for its impact on growth, literacy, child nutrition, and more.

**Co-ordination and long-term commitment are considered important for building partnerships and reducing poverty.** There are no quick solutions for improving the social, political and economic well-being of the poor. "Stop-and-go" policies are considered particularly harmful from both aid effectiveness and poverty reduction perspectives. Good practice, on the other hand, means long-term commitment within a clear, mutually defined framework.

**... and on assessing performance in meeting goals.**

**Development practices and outcomes must be monitored and evaluated to assess partnership performance and to secure and maintain pro-poor effects.** Monitoring is necessary not just to ensure that the desired poverty reduction objectives are being achieved, but also to examine whether development efforts have unintended consequences detrimental to poor people. Evaluation is essential for assessing impact, gauging progress and learning from experience. Monitoring and evaluation should be carried out in partnership with government, local stakeholders and other external agencies.

# The challenges posed by working in partnership

## What does it take to establish good poverty reduction partnerships?

Sound, productive partnerships among governments, civil society and the development community are based on trust, mutual accountability and a shared commitment to the goals, objectives and results to be achieved. They work most effectively when they are based on reciprocal relationships characterised by clear understandings about the roles and responsibilities of each partner and where there is open, inclusive dialogue among them. Key parameters for building effective poverty reduction partnerships are set out in Box 5.

**Working as partners creates challenges such as...**

Working in partnership poses a number of challenges:

- Issues of substantial importance to development agency constituencies (such as environment, gender and governance) must be integrated into policy dialogue *without imposing an externally-driven agenda*.

- Genuine dialogue between central government and other parts of society (for example with local government, the private sector, the organisations of civil society, women's associations and NGOs working on gender issues, and, so far as possible, poor people or their organisations) on local strategies for reducing poverty should be facilitated in ways that *do not undermine the legitimacy of partner governments, the role of parliament and other key democratic institutions*.

- "Development effectiveness" strengthens *the need for a more selective, more strategic approach to aid allocations* based on objective criteria, demonstrated partner performance and a long-term timeframe.

**... not imposing views or priorities on others, promoting open dialogue without undermining governance, and reconciling aid effectiveness with needs and performance.**

Reciprocity is a crucial aspect of working in partnership. Development agencies need to decide collectively, and in collaboration with developing country partners, how they will assess each other's policy commitments, spending plans and contributions to poverty reduction outcomes. Reciprocity of this sort strengthens the trust and commitment of other partners. Performance indicators should increasingly be applied to all partners, with development agencies being called to account – in the same way as governments – for the reliability of their commitments and the consistency of their policies.

## Box 6. Assessing partner government commitment to poverty reduction

Assessing the quality of a country's commitment to reducing poverty calls for difficult qualitative judgements about the pace and scope of change and about government's record in implementing its stated policies. Responses to the following questions may be helpful in assessing the extent and quality of government commitment and in identifying areas where progress is needed or agency support is called for.

- Is there an agreed strategy for reducing poverty and is a medium-term action plan, drawn up in a participatory way, being implemented? Is there a significant role for parliament (or other elected body) and its committees in formulating strategy?

- How representative is stakeholder consultation outside government (for example non-governmental organisations, regions, private sector, press, social groups including women's groups)?

- Is there evidence of a commitment to ensure that work to reduce poverty empowers poor women and increases their opportunities?

- Are plans and budgets transparent, with full publication in a timely way?

- Is there a clear, serious commitment of resources to poverty reduction and is this reflected in the allocation of resources to and within sectors?

- Is adequate weight given to poverty reduction criteria in review procedures for national investment and recurrent expenditure decisions?

- What agreed benchmarks have been achieved by government in implementing the national poverty reduction strategy?

- Does the policy framework distinguish the needs of particular socially or geographically disadvantaged groups? Does it identify specific measures to relieve the constraints they face?

- What incentives are there for government departments to be aware of poverty criteria and respond with improvements in basic services? What incentives are there for officials to work in rural areas, especially those that are remote?

### Gauging commitment and assessing partnership performance

**Criteria for assessing the commitment of partners to poverty reduction.** Partnerships are likely to hinge on the quality of governance and, in particular, on government efforts to orient strategies in a pro-poor, gender-aware direction. Efforts to gauge quality and commitment in these areas must be tailored to specific country contexts (Box 6). Agreement on the criteria used to assess partner performance should be reached at the outset of agency country programming processes.

**Partner countries' performance in achieving partnership goals – such as implementing pro-poor, gender-aware policies and promoting society-wide dialogue – must be continually assessed.**

Other important criteria concern the quality of the policy dialogue and the processes of consultation. As a general rule, accountability to domestic stakeholders, including elected officials, will be critical. Although in practice many national parliaments or legislatures and local assemblies have serious limitations, their existence implies a potential source of pressure against gross misuse of public funds and in support of public spending priorities that reflect government's commitment to reducing poverty. Policy dialogue between government and development agencies should respect the role of parliaments and strengthen local debate and dialogue.

Assessing *continuing* partner commitment to poverty reduction will involve monitoring progress in *implementing* pro-poor policies. This will call for establishing mutually-agreed performance criteria based on benchmarking and quantitative indicators. These should be linked to progress in carrying out the partner country's poverty reduction strategy, including economic reforms underpinning a pro-poor enabling and growth environment.

**Criteria for assessing the performance of development agencies in addressing poverty.** Development agencies should also establish criteria, in co-operation with their partners, for assessing their own performance in supporting poverty reduction partnerships.

Many factors determine successful poverty reduction outcomes, most of which are beyond the scope of bilateral agencies and development assistance more generally. At

---

## Box 7.  Assessing development agency poverty reduction efforts

Working in partnership means giving serious attention to assessing agency performance in measuring up to agreed responsibilities and obligations. The following indicative criteria could be useful in this regard:

- Is the development agency's country strategy based on the partner country's own assessment and strategy for addressing poverty?

- To what extent does the agency's country strategy address the multidimensional aspects of poverty?

- To what extent have the agency's co-operation activities been carried out jointly or in co-ordination with other bilateral and multilateral development agencies (for example missions, appraisals, data collection, analyses, etc.)?

- Allowing for agency constraints, to what extent have agency administrative and financial requirements been adjusted to, or harmonised with, the partner country's existing procedures or with those of other external partners, where these procedures are deemed appropriate?

- To what extent has the agency implemented its support in a manner which respects and fosters partner country ownership?

- Has the agency supported and strengthened country-led planning, implementation and co-ordination processes?

- Has the agency helped to facilitate civil society's participation (at local, national and international level) in debating and deciding the contents of the country's poverty reduction strategy in ways that respect government efforts and concerns?

- Has there been a clear, serious commitment of resources to poverty reduction?

- Has a commitment been made to provide predictable resources over a medium-term planning timeframe?

- Has sufficient care been taken to avoid duplication of effort and to build on complementarities across the external development community?

- Have efforts been made to improve policy coherence within the agency and, more broadly, across the full range of DAC Member government ministries and departments, and has progress been achieved?

---

the same time, a key criterion for evaluating agency performance will be the impact of the development agency's country strategy on progress in achieving sectoral development targets and on improving poverty indicators as set out in each partner country's poverty reduction strategy. This places a premium on developing appropriate evaluation methodologies for assessing poverty reduction *impact*.

Additional criteria might include the extent to which the development agency co-ordinates its planning and implementation activities with other partners, reduces the administrative burden it creates for them and facilitates collaboration (Box 7). Efforts to increase the flexibility and predictability of resources provided – while recognising the constraints on in-kind assistance faced by some development agencies – may also be considered for use as a measure of performance.

Agencies should also assess their performance in terms of the extent to which the projects they support are fully coherent with the partner country's poverty reduction strategy and have been fully integrated in partner government expenditure frameworks.

Harmonising procedures in the partnership mode and improving aid co-ordination are important measures for enhancing the effectiveness of aid in reducing poverty: efforts in this direction should be assessed. Each Member country will have its own comparative advantages and political constraints which will call for some flexibility in arrangements, but with these in mind, it is important for Members to simplify and harmonise financial management and accountability requirements. Simplification and rationalisation of the pre-implementation phase of the project cycle, and reporting and monitoring are also important.

**Development agencies' performance should be assessed as well, including their efforts to achieve poverty goals, streamline administrative requirements and manage the aid process flexibly and rationally.**

The government of each DAC Member should be held responsible for the effectiveness of its aid (for example reducing aid transactions costs, increasing the proportion of local procurement, progress in untying, greater reliance on local experts) as well as its performance in promoting policy coherence across all government departments (especially in development co-operation and trade policies) and in improving access to information and technology (Part 4).

# Strategic approaches for overall development assistance allocation and programming decisions

## The need to allocate more resources to the poorest countries and to the poorest in other developing countries

Given the limited volumes of development assistance and the importance of reducing poverty, it is vital that development co-operation resources are used as effectively as possible. Country allocation criteria need to take into account both the number and share of very poor people and the scope for aid effectiveness in partner countries being considered for support. Maximising development co-operation impact on poverty reduction implies:

**Resources should be allocated according to where aid can be used most effectively to reduce poverty.**

- A concentration on the poorest countries, although some measured and targeted funding should also be provided to other developing countries with widespread poverty.

- Supporting poor populations in medium- and larger-sized countries, where the vast majority of the very poor are found, although aid per capita would remain significantly higher in smaller countries.

- Taking account of lessons of aid effectiveness that highlight the importance of political commitment to fight poverty and an effective policy and institutional environment.

- Ensuring that the partner country's poverty reduction strategy is widely owned, adequate and appropriate.

Poverty continues to be a serious problem in middle-income countries, and development co-operation can play an important, catalytic role in supporting necessary physical and institutional development and mobilising additional development finance for essential social services and private sector-led growth.

## Supporting sound national strategies for reducing poverty

In a general way, the partner country's strategy will determine the nature and extent of agency support. Each country has different needs and capacities for dealing with poverty and has its own view of necessary policies and priorities. Agency support should be tailored accordingly. The legitimacy, adequacy and appropriateness of partner poverty reduction strategies are important criteria to be factored into agency planning and allocation decisions. In some cases, past government performance in implementing policies will also be important.

## The role of development co-operation in different country contexts

Agency country strategies should be adapted to the specific context of each partner country, for example local social and political conditions, the strength and capabilities of national institutions, the depth and breadth of poverty and its geographic and spatial character.

Each partner country presents different, and constantly changing, propensities and opportunities for reducing poverty. This reality makes generalisations or categorisations about what to do in different country contexts difficult and imprecise. Nevertheless, as an organising principle it is helpful to set out an overview of contexts and options, a notional "partner country typology" to help guide agency staff in understanding the role that development co-operation can play in any given country setting. In general, partner countries, despite their considerable differences, will be subject to one of the following sets of circumstances:

**Large and non-aid dependent countries.** The role of development co-operation in reducing poverty in these countries may be marginal given the overall magnitude of macroeconomic balances, access to international capital markets and the fungibility of financial flows. Nevertheless, the needs of the poor – which may be very considerable in some countries – must be addressed and supported. A key priority will be to ensure that development assistance catalyses additional local resources and actions to reduce poverty. In view of the reduced leverage of development co-operation in these countries, efforts to foster greater commitment and resources for reducing poverty should focus on dialogue with partners, advocacy and efforts to strengthen the voice of civil society in policy formulation. In countries with federal structures, it may be possible to work sub-nationally. Entry points for assistance include *poverty-focused support* for developing the private sector (for example micro-finance and business management skills, especially for women), upgrading public sector performance, improving governance structures and institutions (including at the sub-national level) and promoting policy coherence across Member country governments (especially trade, agriculture and financial policies). There is also a case for development assistance to test new and innovative approaches to poverty reduction on an experimental basis.

**Countries that have developed a poverty reduction strategy but lack local implementation capacity.** In countries with a policy environment that functions reasonably well and where efforts to overcome the remaining shortfalls are being made, development agency strategies and programmes should be a subset of the country-led strategy and public investment priorities. It will be important to agree on how to account satisfactorily for results and outcomes of external financing without distorting national spending priorities. Agencies assessing their support for countries in economic transition should factor in the time required for social and economic change. Key areas for assistance for these countries include public sector institutional development (at the national, regional and municipal level), civil society capacity-building and technical co-operation for sectoral development.

**Countries striving to develop economic strategies and social policies for poverty reduction that lack capacity and institutional mechanisms.** In countries still striving to articulate a coherent poverty reduction strategy, process indicators and intermediate measures of progress towards goals are particularly important. Context-specific process indicators – including whether and how representatives of poor or vulnerable groups have been able to participate – can help in assessing the degree of commitment to poverty reduction. Development agency programming in these countries should encourage domestic participation in analysing poverty. Members should help to strengthen the capacity of these countries to analyse and interpret data, particularly social, economic and political data that bear upon gender inequality and other forms of disempowerment and social exclusion. If countries are committed to poverty reduction but are unable to articulate this, action to strengthen analytical capacity should be complemented by resource transfers in the form of support to country-led projects. It may also be possible to support sector-wide approaches in some areas and to provide debt relief, foreign exchange or investment resources. Advocacy and policy dialogue on poverty issues are also areas for agency support.

> A "partner county typology" has been developed to help agency staff understand what policy options and types of support are best in a given set of circumstances.

> Where a partner country has not yet concluded its thinking and consultations on a poverty reduction strategy, intermediate measures of progress will be important in assessing the extent of its commitment to reducing poverty.

**Countries recovering from conflict or natural disaster.** In countries emerging from conflict or natural disasters, development agencies may focus on restoring damaged economic infrastructure and basic services to mitigate the impact of such calamities on the poor. In these situations, reducing the risks, vulnerability and insecurity associated with being poor can be part and parcel of emergency relief, rehabilitation or peace-building efforts. At the same time, while a credible commitment or track record on poverty reduction may be missing for such countries, development assistance (particularly capacity-building support) may be critical to creating the space that would allow governments to begin to focus on poverty reduction needs. Development agencies should also consider supporting media and civil society for building alliances for poverty reduction (particularly where countries are emerging from conflict) and to local projects focused on improving governance.

**Agency support will be constrained in countries where there is conflict, poor governance, or lack of commitment to reducing poverty.**

**Countries where government is not demonstrating adequate commitment to poverty reduction.** In countries where weak governance, conflict, or a government not committed to reducing poverty prevail, the kinds of support development agencies can provide may be severely limited. Serious concerns about governance, human rights and the effectiveness of aid will prevent government-to-government co-operation. Agencies can then only work with local authorities or through non-governmental organisations (NGOs) to help relieve poverty among particular, targeted populations. They can also provide more general support to reduce vulnerability and to satisfy humanitarian needs. Where governance is absent or very weak, community-based approaches may be the only possible response. Finally, bilateral agencies could consider how their support for local structures, civil society and the private sector could foster "pathways" for more serious partner country commitment to poverty reduction and development agency engagement in the future.

Agencies should bear in mind the importance, in all country contexts, of sustaining and learning from local civil society relations. Strong engagement with civil society will provide essential feedback for assessing the political dimensions of local poverty reduction in relation to the interests of élites and local leadership, and understanding government accountability to, and interaction with, the poor.

### Dealing with dilemma situations

**Helping partners in severe difficulty.** There are other developmental objectives in aid allocations beyond poverty reduction. These include conflict prevention, human rights and participatory democracy, gender equality and sustainable development. There is also often an acute need to help countries adjust to external shocks, for example refugees from conflicts in neighbouring countries, natural disasters, or terms-of-trade shocks – all of which affect economic and social development performance.

**What should bilateral agencies do when a partner country does not comply, or only partially complies, with commitments or responsibilities they have agreed to undertake?**

**Collaborate closely with other external partners in dealing with dilemma situations.** Countries with inadequate development policies and institutions need support to create conditions enabling performance to improve. Working as partners with such countries in ways that promote country ownership – and yet that ensure aid is effective and has poverty reduction impact – is likely to be problematical. What happens when a partner government does not comply, or only partially complies, with its stated intentions or commitments? Policy conditions – often bundled with financial and technical support – have sometimes helped reform-minded (usually new) governments advance reform agendas. But externally-imposed conditionality has generally not been effective, sustainable or conducive to country ownership and is least likely to work in countries lacking the basis for partnership. Emerging good practice suggests the following approaches:

- A moderate share of assistance should be reserved for these countries.
- External partners should have a shared view as regards the partner country and co-ordinate their development co-operation and other actions and policies.

- Assistance should be used to support sustainable national or local institutions and civil society, with an emphasis on addressing the barriers to adequate performance: this includes renewed policy dialogue, supporting local coalitions for reform and strengthening local capacity for research and social dialogue.

- Development co-operation could also support local authorities and NGOs in relieving poverty among targeted populations to reduce vulnerability and to satisfy humanitarian needs.

Judgements about how to proceed in a dilemma would best be worked out among all agencies involved in the partner country concerned. It will be important to react promptly and decisively. Helpful actions include policy dialogue, working to build consensus among external partners, supporting local coalitions for reform, and strengthening local research capacity and social dialogue. Assessing partner countries' performance in implementing their poverty reduction strategy will enable agencies to determine future eligibility for assistance and the type of assistance to be provided. Good performers can be expected to receive more programme support. Countries that are not performing well can expect assistance to be more circumscribed (for example it will be targeted, channelled through specific intermediaries, focused on capacity-building). This will have an unavoidable impact on the volume of assistance, since transaction costs and delays for agencies providing assistance under these conditions are higher.

> **Partner countries that perform well can expect to receive more programmatic support, while poor performers can expect assistance to be more closely circumscribed – which will necessarily have an impact on aid volume.**

## Helping partners to develop sound national poverty reduction strategies

### Policy dialogue – a key locus of partner interaction

The process of in-country policy dialogue is an integral element in ongoing efforts to establish strong, effective partnerships for reducing poverty. It is the arena in which the views and concerns that all partners have about poverty reduction issues and the choices to be made must be debated and agreed. In general, agreements and decisions reached during the dialogue about economic, political and administrative reforms in partner countries will determine the terms of agency engagement. In order to negotiate effectively with local counterparts, agencies should be well informed about local poverty.

> **The views and concerns of different actors and stakeholders about poverty reduction strategy issues and choices must be debated and reconciled.**

The policy dialogue should build confidence and forge longer-term partnerships around shared objectives. As regards poverty reduction, this implies a more integrated and holistic dialogue combining diverse policies and programmes at national, sector and local levels as a way of addressing the different dimensions of poverty and its causes. The main issues and concerns to be discussed in a poverty-focused policy dialogue include support for pro-poor growth (economic and structural policies and sustainable livelihood approaches), measures to promote equity, social inclusion and human development (gender mainstreaming, better quality and reach of basic social services) and governance and institutional changes that create an enabling environment for reducing poverty (empowerment, rights and pro-poor governance).[1]

In the short term, especially in those countries still in transition towards a fully articulated poverty reduction strategy with effective implementing institutions, intense dialogue between development agencies and countries is likely to remain necessary. Without this, priorities and performance cannot be expected to move in a more pro-poor, gender-aware direction.

> **Agencies and partner governments should agree at an early stage on benchmarks for assessing progress towards reaching poverty reduction goals.**

---

1. See Part 1, "Why policy actions are required?".

Partner country poverty reduction strategies will contain implicit partner government commitments and responsibilities against which other partners can measure performance in terms of policy change and structural reforms. Agencies and their partner governments should aim to agree on relevant objectives and on benchmarks for assessing progress towards reaching those objectives.

### Agency support for national anti-poverty strategies

Assistance is often required in elaborating national anti-poverty strategies and action plans. The nature and timing of such assistance can be crucial. Examples of appropriate assistance include:

- Help in diagnosing the nature and causes of poverty so as to permit the most effective design of public actions, including better understanding of gender-specific issues and the implications for vulnerable groups.

- Support for developing guidelines for poverty-focused sector-wide and integrated programmes that promote decentralisation and an active role for local communities.

- Resources for monitoring and evaluating poor people's access to services within sector-wide programmes.

- Strengthening capacity for generating and analysing information and statistics, including support for poverty assessments and the development of relevant statistical techniques and tools (for example data that have been disaggregated by gender, age, social group, etc.).

- Facilitating and building capacity for broader public participation in creating poverty reduction strategies by, for example, helping civil society organisations and women get involved in consultations and supporting the work of parliamentary or legislative committees or independent public policy institutes.

- Reinforcing the capacities of partner country in managing and accounting for aid flows and in assessing impact and promoting institutional learning.

- Strengthening capacity at decentralised and local levels to allow maximum voice for strengthening local ownership of the country's poverty reduction strategy.

**It is crucial for partner countries to be given the time and the "space" they need to develop their own, widely shared, poverty reduction strategies.**

Every effort should be expended to ensure that partner country authorities are given adequate time and space to develop their own, widely shared, poverty reduction strategies.

Development agency technical co-operation should be based on minimum intervention. Activities should be planned and implemented by the developing country (to the maximum extent possible), and should genuinely contribute to national capacity-building and the promotion of local expertise. This includes studies underpinning national poverty reduction strategies. Agencies should ensure close co-operation with partner governments and clear agreement on tasks and responsibilities of expatriate advisors who should be directly accountable to government. Care should be taken to ensure that work is undertaken in accordance with local priorities and that information generated through development assistance is shared with all stakeholders and parties involved. To fulfil its facilitatory function, technical co-operation offers a wide range of instruments, such as local and international experts on a short- or long-term basis, which can be combined with financial assistance.

### Strengthening the empirical foundations of poverty reduction strategies

National poverty reduction strategies should be based on the best available knowledge about poverty. Concerted efforts are needed to strengthen local capacity for generating and managing data for diagnostic analysis and policy prescription. To this end, development agencies could provide direct and indirect support to build skills and knowledge and to mediate between partner countries and regional or international institutions. Sectors to benefit from such interaction include food security (early warning systems), agriculture, fisheries, environment (satellite data) and health.

The critical and analytical use of data is a weak area for partner countries and agencies alike. It is necessary to match development agency concerns about gender equality with better empirical and gender-disaggregated data in order to produce country-specific analyses of poverty-gender links and to shape proactive gender policies. Similar analyses are required for environment-poverty links.

At the same time, partnership considerations argue for two priorities:

- Sharing openly and regularly with partner governments, civil society (South and North) and other development agencies all analytical work, which should be used to develop *collective or shared poverty assessments*.

- Working closely with country institutions at all levels – thereby taking advantage of scarce skills, benefiting from synergies and promoting active learning – to develop *common diagnostic frameworks*.

### Collaborating with other partners

**Casting the net wide.** In every developing country there is a host of existing and potential partners whose diverse talents, capacities and energies could strengthen the fight against poverty. Central ministries, local government, self-help groups, civil society organisations (from both North and South), trade unions, opposition movements, women's organisations, the private sector, the research community, religious groups, bilateral and multilateral development agencies, and poor people themselves – all these groups should participate in designing, funding and implementing poverty reduction strategies. Engaging all potential partners in a co-ordinated, concerted effort should be the goal.

**The political reality of poverty reduction.** Efforts to undertake pro-poor structural and policy reforms in partner countries are bound to take on political overtones given inevitable tensions between groups clinging to privileges and rents, and groups that are more amenable to pursuing reform and to implementing pro-poor policies. By engaging in development co-operation, agencies cannot avoid being drawn into these tensions. Agencies must be aware that dealing with a range of partners in a given economic, social and political context where the pursuit of poverty reduction objectives may not be fully shared by all stakeholders will present challenges for which there are no straightforward solutions. Supporting government efforts to engage society in dialogue on development options and choices will enable agencies to improve their understanding of local social and political dynamics, and to build strategic alliances and partnerships with reform-minded individuals and institutions. Efforts to establish pluralistic, participatory democracies wherein the poor can exercise "voice" will most effectively address this challenge. Additional useful actions could include support parliaments or legislatures, independent media, policy research institutions and civil society organisations.

**Making the most of partner contributions.** Clarity about the relative strengths and comparative advantages of different partners can help to focus their efforts most effectively. For example, civil society organisations can play a key role in mobilising local actors, catalysing self-help efforts, channelling additional resources, advocating empowerment and participation, and reaching out to marginalised groups and communities. The private sector has a role to play as the primary sector for creating sustainable jobs, providing resources for development and promoting the transfer of technology and know-how. Labour organisations can help to promote decent work and improve working conditions. Multilateral agencies can contribute research capacity, resource flows and broader global

*Collective or shared poverty assessments and common diagnostic frameworks should be a priority area of joint effort between external agencies and local authorities.*

*Pro-poor structural change and policy reform are inherently political – and often controversial. Agencies should work to support social dialogue, reform-minded institutions and individuals, and information flows.*

and regional exchange and interaction. Bilateral agencies can contribute their strong field presence, long-standing relationships with government and local actors, additional resources and experience with political development and governance.

**The key role of community organisations.** Non-governmental organisations and private sector-based entities such as chambers of commerce and the enterprise sector can spearhead effective and innovative initiatives for reducing poverty and should receive the institutional and financial support they require for implementing such activities. Many NGOs, for example, have pioneered "good practice" in developing informal learning and literacy methodologies, and in such areas as peace-building, strategic gender programming, partnerships with local government and capacity-building of local civil society organisations. Supporting the advocacy, lobbying and networking activities of local NGOs representing the poor is essential to creating and maintaining an enabling environment for poverty reduction by giving "voice" to the poor. Key challenges for improving the effectiveness of these social actors include strengthening their administrative capacity, building their analytical capacity and extending their reach to the very poorest segments of society.

**Partnership means dialogue beyond government.** Many partners decry the exclusive nature of poverty debates in their countries. More partners, and a broader range of partners, should be engaged in the policy dialogue running alongside efforts to formulate and implement strategies for reducing poverty. Extra effort will be required to ensure the quality of these consultation processes in the sense of *ensuring genuine,* ex ante *participation that informs outcomes*. Agencies can provide support for this essential dialogue by backstopping the logistics, planning, information-gathering, facilitation, co-ordination and dissemination required for different dialogues.

> **Extra efforts will be needed to ensure that government/ civil society consultations on poverty issues are genuine exchanges that shape ultimate policy choices.**

In supporting government efforts to foster broader local participation in the dialogue, agencies must exercise care not to undermine the legitimacy of partner governments and to identify *bona fide* agents of civil society who can legitimately speak for the poor. The overriding need to respect partner efforts to build and consolidate their own constitutional and democratic institutions must be emphasised. Efforts to build more open relationships with civil society are especially important in countries where government policy is still considered unfavourable, or where there is as yet an ill-defined country-led poverty reduction strategy. In other situations, it is important from the point of view of strengthening government accountability to society at large.

> **Working with local partners and stakeholders is time-consuming, labour-intensive and risky, the more so given agency programming, staffing and budget constraints.**

**Genuine participation of local stakeholders is a challenge.** Working with local partners and stakeholders is time-consuming, labour-intensive and risky (for example it may not lead to the expected results). Participation may be very difficult to facilitate and to manage given rigid programming and budget pressures that continue to prevail in development co-operation programmes and projects. At the same time, it is essential for ensuring ownership, sustainability and effectiveness. The participation and empowerment of women, socially marginalised and excluded groups, and the poorest of the poor must be squarely addressed by development agencies. Effective systems of monitoring and feedback are required to secure the participation of these groups. In a larger sense, agencies should support partner governments' efforts to institutionalise participation throughout societies, building up participatory processes and mechanisms that will facilitate efforts to *scale up* participation beyond local levels.

> **Bilateral agencies can interact more effectively with multilateral partners by becoming more proactive in analysing multilateral policies and challenging those that adversely affect the poor.**

**Engaging more effectively with multilateral partners.** Agencies need to work more closely and more collegially with multilateral partners, both at the corporate level through interactions in their decision-making bodies and in the field (Box 8). Effective collaboration will require bilateral agencies to become more proactive in analysing the policies of multilateral institutions and to be prepared to challenge these institutions when their policies adversely affect the poor.

### Box 8. How bilateral agencies can work most effectively with multilateral institutions

Several bilateral agencies consider collaboration with multilateral and regional institutions as an important way of leveraging the scope and impact of their assistance programmes. Closer and more supportive relationships among external partners are an important goal for all concerned, especially in the context of nationally-driven processes and strategic frameworks. Options here include:

- Identifying and agreeing with multilateral institutions the respective roles, responsibilities and obligations of the different external partners in country-specific poverty reduction strategy processes.

- Establishing feedback channels from the field to headquarters informing management of implementation opportunities, challenges and problems.

- Participating actively in bilateral and multilateral forums for co-ordinating assistance (for example Strategic Partnership with Africa, Consultative Groups, Round Tables).

- Where possible, providing predictable, transparent and longer-term commitment of resources to support joint poverty reduction efforts with multilateral institutions.

- Being aware of missions and opportunities for policy dialogue and initiating early and prompt contact with relevant multilateral staff.

- Keeping periodic co-ordination meetings informal, operational and focused on results (for example share experience, discuss options and possible scenarios, seek advice, co-ordinate activities and research).

- Looking for ways to streamline and simplify funding and disbursement arrangements (for example having each development agency volunteer to fund a certain percentage of a programme, with the government providing periodic financial reports).

- Identifying and managing technical assistance co-operation among bilateral and multilateral institutions.

### Supporting national poverty reduction strategies through better aid co-ordination

**Co-ordination issues.** Aid co-ordination in the context of partnership is the joint responsibility of all partners, although it should be initiated and led by partner governments.[2] Bilateral agencies must make determined and sustained efforts to share information and work together with a view to delivering coherent and consistent messages and focusing on essential needs and collaboration opportunities. At the same time, it is vital for multilateral agencies to share information with other partners in order to catalyse genuine co-ordination and enable other partners to use their frameworks to fullest advantage. Increased delegation of decision-making to field offices will provide the impetus and margin of manoeuvre necessary for spurring more and better co-operation and co-ordination in the field. This co-ordination should include bilateral and multilateral agencies at country, regional and international levels.

The challenge for the development community is to find ways of collaborating that do not undermine country ownership nor create additional burdens for partner countries.

At the same time, agencies must pay closer attention to consistency across the development community and within their own agencies (whether they are composed of single or multiple government departments or agencies). Greater coherence between development agencies and their fellow government ministries represented on the boards of multilateral institutions is essential for reducing the risk of conflicting approaches and improving the internal coherence in DAC Members' overall development policy and their efforts to reduce poverty. Each agency must remain vigilant to risks of inconsistency, duplication and overlap with other external partners – and within their own agencies –

**The challenge facing development agencies is finding ways of collaborating that do not undermine ownership nor create additional burdens for partner countries.**

---

2. In this enabling context, the Poverty Reduction Strategy, national budget and medium-term fiscal review processes are important mechanisms for structuring and co-ordinating development assistance (Part 3).

in both policy dialogue and programming. Greater harmonisation of development agency practices at bilateral, regional and international levels is required, but this needs the commitment by all agencies to work together to maximise comparative advantage, to identify the best allocation of scarce resources and to ensure overall coherence in the delivery of development assistance to the partner country concerned.

Consultative groups and round tables are mechanisms for aid co-ordination that can simultaneously strengthen partner country capacity and ownership. The partner country should drive these forums while ensuring a prominent place for the poverty reduction agenda. Efforts should be made to support partner country venues for these meetings, and high-level agency headquarters staff should participate.

## Priority actions for the bilateral community

Part 2 has set out the basic principles of partnership and described how agencies can apply them in diverse country situations as they help partners develop and implement sound national strategies for reducing poverty.

**Agency priorities for building poverty reduction partnerships include:**

DAC Members have assessed these ideas and identified a number of priorities for agency action, particularly at the field level. These include stronger commitments to:

**... supporting country-owned, country-led poverty reduction strategies,...**

- *Support country-owned, country-led strategies for reducing poverty* and base agency programming on needs and priorities identified in these strategies.

- *Allocate more development assistance to countries where there is greatest scope for reducing poverty* given the number of absolute poor, the strength of government commitment to tackle poverty and demonstrated policy performance.

**... allocating resources where greatest impact on poverty can be achieved,...**

- *Reduce the burden development assistance creates for local partners* by combining efforts (for example joint missions, collaborative research, common diagnostics, shared costs), easing administrative requirements (for example simplifying, streamlining and, where practicable, harmonising paperwork and procedures; accepting partner design for strategies and documents wherever possible), and co-ordinating agency approaches and actions.

- *Invest the time and resources needed* to build genuine, reciprocal poverty reduction partnerships and to sustain them through mechanisms and networks that are cost-effective and efficient.

**... streamlining and simplifying aid management and working together on similar tasks,...**

- *Adapt development agency structures and working methods* to the challenges and needs of poverty reduction partnerships (for example by strengthening and deepening field presence, enhancing decision-making flexibility, accepting partner design for documents and strategies, increasing transparency and accountability to other partners, lengthening programming timeframes and developing staff "facilitation" and consensus-building skills).

**... strengthening local institutional capacity to implement policies and manage aid flows,...**

- Work more intensively to *develop human and institutional capacity* (for example improving governance and promoting empowerment, enabling partners to manage and account for development assistance, promoting the use of information and communication technology, etc.).

- *Ensure a gender perspective* in all policies, programmes, instruments and modalities (as opposed to having a discrete section on gender implications).

- *Integrate sustainable development*, including environmental concerns, in poverty reduction strategic frameworks.

- Adopt, to the greatest extent possible, a *multi-year timeframe* for poverty reduction programming and funding as a complement to multi-year partner government fiscal planning and budgeting.

- Assess development co-operation performance in terms of *poverty reduction reach and impact*, and set up the requisite monitoring and evaluation systems and methodologies.

- *Foster and strengthen local efforts* (for example civil society, parliaments and legislatures, government bodies) to monitor poverty reduction programmes and the use of debt relief.

- Encourage countries to develop *local poverty reduction indicators and targets* and strengthen partners' statistical, analytical and *evaluation capacity*.

**... increasing resource transfer flexibility and timeframes...**

**... and assessing agency performance in terms of poverty reduction impact.**

# **3** Frameworks and instruments for country programming

## Introduction

Country programming processes and choices have a central role to play in poverty reduction. Part 3 outlines evolving partner country frameworks for shaping, implementing and monitoring national strategies linked to poverty reduction goals. It describes the changing role of bilateral agency country strategies for enhancing the focus and impact of country operations on reducing poverty. Finally, it reviews the relative merits of key development co-operation instruments and emerging good practice in increasing aid effectiveness for poverty reduction.

## The evolving partner country strategy framework

Approaches to country programming should, first and foremost, build on partner country strategic frameworks and planning instruments. These national frameworks should serve the purpose of framing policies, setting priorities, converting them into spending decisions, and monitoring outcomes in relation to poverty reduction. This section differentiates a number of development frameworks in partner countries that the international community has been supporting in recent years. And it identifies specific challenges for development agencies co-operating through these instruments.

**Country-led development frameworks are essential tools for integrating economic, social and environmental priorities...**

### Country-level strategic development frameworks

There is widespread agreement in the international community on the need to evolve comprehensive, country-led development frameworks that integrate national anti-poverty strategies. This has led international bodies to propose several closely related, often interlocking frameworks. These include the National Strategies for Sustainable Development (NSSD) from the United Nations Conference on Environment and Development in 1992; the United Nations Development Assistance Framework's Common Country Assessment (UNDAF/CCA) introduced as a pilot in 1997; the World Bank Comprehensive Development Framework (CDF) initiated in early 1999; and the Poverty Reduction Strategy Paper processes (PRSP) launched by the Bretton Woods institutions in late 1999.

Taken together these frameworks, in their various national adaptations, are strategic tools for translating national and international development goals into policy action. Efforts should be made to ensure that the frameworks are comprehensive, support poverty reduction, and are consistent with other national strategies. In a best case scenario, partner countries would have a single national plan integrating economic, social and environmental priorities in a holistic strategic policy framework geared to ensuring that overall development – including poverty reduction – will be sustainable.[1]

**... in a holistic strategy geared to reduce poverty.**

Recognising the added burden for partner countries of having to comply with multiple frameworks, the international community should rationalise the various documents and economic plans currently being prepared by partners, international organisations and bilateral agencies. Development agencies should support the formulation of national strategies by strengthening local capacity for designing policy, for carrying out consultation processes and conducting relevant research and analysis (Part 2). Strategies developed in these frameworks, and particularly the country-led poverty reduction strategy, should be the point of departure for agency country-based poverty reduction programming and activities.

### Country-led poverty reduction strategy processes

There are a number of challenges related to the widespread adoption of a country-led poverty reduction strategy (PRS) approach: ownership and commitment by the partner country, its capacity to develop prioritised action plans and the capacity of civil society to engage with government (as well as the willingness of government to engage with civil society), the quality and availability of poverty data, and the challenges of identifying pro-poor growth paths. There is also a particular opportunity to promote the better integration of environmental sustainability issues into the emerging strategies for poverty reduction. Country-led PRS should evolve into long-term sustainable strategies.

In those instances where low-income countries are required to develop Poverty Reduction Strategy Papers (PRSPs) in the context of the Enhanced HIPC (Heavily Indebted Poor Countries) initiative and in seeking concessional assistance from the World Bank and the International Monetary Fund (IMF), it is expected that PRSPs should support and improve, but not duplicate or undermine, national poverty reduction policy processes.

**The poverty reduction strategy should be country-driven, participatory, comprehensive and results-oriented.**

The poverty reduction strategy should be country-driven, based on participatory processes, comprehensive in scope, and results-oriented. In supporting the PRS processes – relatively new and largely untested – development agencies should be attentive to the following issues: different formats and standards should be accepted; the pace of the PRS process needs to be adapted to suit country capacity and to allow more local ownership to develop. It should not be influenced by disbursement pressure. PRS requirements should be flexible and adapted to a long-term process as sustained poverty reduction cannot be achieved overnight. The process should be open to bilateral agencies to participate in an integrated way according to their comparative advantages with respect to planning, implementation, monitoring and evaluation of the poverty reduction strategy.

### National budgets and public expenditure reviews

The national (or sub-national) budget is a most important tool for prioritisation and accountability in achieving the objectives set out in the national poverty reduction strategy. It is an annual expenditure and revenue plan, which has the advantage of reflecting government policy priorities, costed plans for achieving particular outcomes, and the total resource envelope considered consistent with macroeconomic stability. Where appropriate, development agency funding commitments should be fully reflected in the budget, thus ensuring greater transparency in the allocation of external resources and allowing the government to set priorities for a larger share of development assistance. In this context, public expenditure reviews conducted in partnership with external agencies are crucial to ensuring pro-poor use of resources, rationalising the size of government and targeting vulnerable groups.

## Medium-term fiscal reviews

In partner countries with the capacity to put together a medium-term fiscal review, agencies may rely on this country-owned, forward-looking instrument. A medium-term fiscal review is potentially helpful to poverty reduction because it links more closely the goals of the national poverty reduction strategy with revenues and expenditures, and at the same time creates the basis for the annual budgeting processes. It is a tool that can greatly enhance accountability if indicators are established and transparent processes developed to show whether spending has served the intended beneficiaries.

Periodic fiscal reviews may become important stocktaking exercises, giving governments and their partners a chance to review jointly their shared commitments to reducing poverty. But the medium-term fiscal framework is only one of several important tools for reducing poverty. It does not focus on results or such off-budget issues as development policies or the role of the private sector.

Initial experience with country-led poverty reduction strategies has emphasised the need for longer-term commitments from development agencies. Where policies permit, development agencies should be willing to use the fiscal reviews to signal the intended continuity of their assistance.

# Development agency country strategies

The trend in partner countries towards developing strategic frameworks for reducing poverty should help focus development agency programming. The long-term goal should be for agency country strategies to diminish in importance. In best-case circumstances the agency strategy will be a "business plan" for the implementation of partner-led national strategies for reducing poverty. In the interim, agencies will rely on their agency-specific planning frameworks when they need to organise and fit their assistance within a given partner country context.

Essential requirements for developing a poverty-focused country strategy stem from the basic principles outlined in Parts 1 and 2. Specifically, country strategies should:

- Focus on poverty reduction goals, including pro-poor economic growth, and be justified in terms of these, with appropriate senior management screening.

- Be aligned with the partner country's strategy for reducing poverty, which should be the template for programming and implementation by all partners.

- Reflect knowledge of what other development agencies are doing in the country and what aid co-ordination mechanisms exist.

- Be genuinely strategic and informed by the best available knowledge of the poverty situation in the country, including the results of poverty assessments, gender and social analysis, and consideration of environment-poverty linkages (Box 9).

*The partner country's poverty reduction strategy should be the template for programming and implementation by all development agencies.*

---

**Box 9. Possible model for a bilateral development agency poverty-focused country strategy**

1. The country's poverty profile (nature, causes, dynamics, identification/location of the poor).

2. Description and assessment of the country's commitment to poverty reduction.

3. Summary of key elements of the country strategy for sustainable poverty reduction (for example sectors, governance, participation/consultation, and targets, indicators, monitoring and evaluation).

4. Proposed development agency strategy:

   Issues for the policy dialogue (priorities, responsibilities, performance, governance, etc.).

   Review of relevant "lessons learned" and good practice from inside and outside the agency.

   Components of support (justify in view of national poverty reduction strategy, development agency comparative advantage, relevant capacity strengthening efforts):

   – Pro-poor economic growth: pace and quality.

   – Empowerment, rights and pro-poor governance.

   – Basic social services for human development.

   – Human security: reducing vulnerability and managing shocks.

   – Mainstreaming gender and enhancing gender equality.

   – Mainstreaming environmental sustainability using sustainable livelihood approaches.

   Modes of intervention and their financing:

   – Balance between direct/indirect focus on poor people (including targeting mechanisms), indirect or inclusive actions for broad groups of people including the poor (for example Sector-Wide Approaches (SWAps) and wider structural actions to underpin pro-poor growth.

   – Balance between budget support (general budget, poverty funds, sector support) and project grants or lending taking into account the debt sustainability prospects.

   Co-ordination mechanisms (government, external development agencies, local stakeholders).

5. Policy coherence issues.

6. Country performance indicators (as far as possible taken from a common set of indicators agreed between development agencies and the partner government).

7. Development agency country strategy self-evaluation benchmarks (clear, monitorable and time-bound benchmarks to track implementation).

---

*Note: Statements 1–3 to be taken directly from the partner country's poverty reduction strategy documents.*

## Policy areas for poverty-focused co-operation

Poverty-focused development co-operation, in whatever form – programme aid, sector support, projects, technical co-operation or policy dialogue – should address the key policy areas identified in Part 1. Following are examples of the kind of reforms undertaken by partner countries, which deserve particular support from a poverty reduction perspective.

*Governance reforms deserve particular support from a poverty reduction perspective.*

**Support for good governance** is an area where bilateral agencies can play a strong role in supporting social inclusion through participation, increased accountability, reduced corruption and increased efficiency in public sector management. The main issues for governance in reducing poverty are ensuring that both poor men and women have greater influence in policy-making and greater access to basic services of decent quality. In this respect, increasing women's access requires specific attention, strategies and resources.

**Public service reform** to improve efficiency in public sector management and services is critical for the design and implementation of pro-poor policies. Reform should strengthen accountability by selecting, appointing and promoting civil servants on merit, developing and enforcing codes of conduct, scrutinising government policies and performance through elected bodies, and monitoring and reporting on the effectiveness and quality of service delivery. Reform should also encourage inclusion – opening public offices to meet public need, instituting new approaches to consulting people living in poverty and setting minimum equitable and affordable standards for basic services.

**Fiscal management reforms** are crucial in promoting a pro-poor allocation of resources across and within sectors, regions and population groups. Reform measures particularly relevant to reducing poverty include: *i)* tax and customs administrations, which are key to improving governance, maintaining economic stability, and, not least, increasing resources that can be channelled towards the poor; *ii)* institutional reforms, such as tax legislation, setting up revenue authorities, public expenditure reviews, improved treasury management, and strengthening public accounts offices, and *iii)* tax policy reforms leading to more effective resource allocation by improving the tax collection effectiveness and the distributional incidence of taxes.

**Decentralisation** can raise the quality of, and access to, services that benefit the poor. It allows closer involvement of the representatives of the poor in public policy, thereby enhancing its pro-poor nature, its accountability and the sustainability of its outcomes. It also supports legitimate devolution of powers under federated political systems. It increases local sense of ownership and helps adjust plans to local realities. But decentralisation also involves some risks that should not be underestimated: local government can be captured by local élites, regional disparities can be deepened, or central government can "disown" responsibility for the poor. The extent and phasing of decentralisation need to take into account the special national, and sometimes sub-national, circumstances in any given country, including the need for keeping an appropriate balance among levels, involving relevant stakeholders and assessing local capacity. Technical co-operation may help mediate conflicts of interests and strengthen capacities across the various groups of stakeholders involved.

**Land tenure reform** is necessary for reducing poverty in many agrarian economies, requiring legislative action to strengthen property rights and remove the gender bias. Land reform is a highly sensitive area. Where politically feasible, it can go a long way in achieving a more equitable distribution of assets. Good practice includes the use of market-based instruments; introducing legislation on security of tenure; fostering public-private partnerships to support agricultural production with training, credit and technology; and linking land reform to decentralisation.

**Support for civil society** is vital in reducing poverty. Bilateral agencies have a comparative advantage in promoting pluralism in civil society by supporting professional associations (such as small farmers associations, trade unions) and human rights organisations. These local organisations can be influential agents of change, well suited to address the needs and interests of politically marginalised groups (ethnic minorities, women, landless farmers, slum-dwellers). Supporting a constituency for human rights is critical for both empowering poor people to improve their living conditions and for enabling civil society to criticise and redress unjust or inefficient policies. This is particularly important for women in their fight against discrimination. Independent media will greatly facilitate these processes. Policy dialogue, especially at the highest political and administrative levels, is an appropriate avenue for raising human rights issues and specific government actions and policy reforms.

**Private sector development** is also critical given the poverty-reducing potential of a dynamic private sector, which can generate employment, wealth and know-how, and integrate women and other disadvantaged groups into economic life. Development agencies may support measures to create a favourable legal environment, reduce administrative and regulatory barriers to investment, strengthen the financial sector and foster the privatisation of state-owned enterprises under competitive conditions. Tailored approaches may ensure a more pro-poor orientation and impact. For example, the proceeds of privatisation can be used to finance micro-enterprise funds for redundant workers, support micro-finance institutions or develop infrastructure that benefit the informal sector and poorer segments of the population.

Country political analyses assessing the political impact of policies and programmes are essential in selecting areas for support.

# Key instruments of financial and technical co-operation

Development agencies rely on different instruments of co-operation to help partner countries reduce poverty. These include national, regional or sector programmes and projects, which are generally combined with policy dialogue at each level and backed up with technical co-operation. In difficult situations or special circumstances, debt relief, humanitarian assistance or support for regional co-operation may also be provided.

**Given important synergies, development agencies should rely on a mix of instruments combining programme aid, sector support and projects with policy dialogue and technical co-operation.**

Given the diversity of contexts in partner countries, it is not possible to say that one form of development co-operation will, in all cases, have a greater impact on poverty reduction than another. But in the right political, economic and institutional environment, programme aid may be an effective delivery mode to reduce poverty on a large scale, if supported by substantial aid volumes. Projects, which affect a limited number of people, can make a lasting impact on the livelihoods of beneficiaries provided they are financially sustainable and compatible with the macro-framework. The focus of development agencies on reducing poverty has rekindled a strategic debate on the relative merits of programme and project aid. This is leading to a growing emphasis on supporting sector programmes and a shift towards maximising the effectiveness of local projects recognising the key role of country ownership.

Given the important synergies that can be achieved by combining different types of development co-operation at the macro, meso and micro levels, country programming ideally should consist of a mix of instruments. The choice of instruments and the balance among direct and indirect, wider and focused actions should flow from an analysis of the country's needs, elicited through a dialogue with government and other stakeholders as outlined in Part 2.

### Programme aid

Programme aid consists of financial contributions extended to a partner country for general development purposes such as balance of payment support or budget support, not linked to specific project activities. It is often associated with the promotion of policy reforms at the macroeconomic level and/or in specific sectors.

**Programme aid can open the way to a continuing dialogue on pro-poor policies in the critical areas of macroeconomic reforms and good governance.**

The role of programme aid in reducing poverty is to provide financial resources, in the most efficient way possible, to a country that is committed and operationally able to using them effectively to implement a sound strategy for reducing poverty. It is a form of development co-operation that signals the readiness of the development agency to respond to improved policies by recognising the partner country's responsibility for financial decisions and management. It substantially reduces the transaction costs, incurred in other donor procedures, that may unduly strain the administrative capacities of partner countries. Quick disbursement, a unique feature of programme support, also helps to meet the partners' immediate financing needs where macroeconomic stability, as well as programmes important to reducing poverty, would otherwise be threatened.

Programme aid assumes good framework conditions in partner countries. It may be usefully complemented by specific projects or technical co-operation that aim to strengthen the capacity of governments to undertake governance reforms, including enhancing accountability, and to implement programmes for poverty reduction. Given the fungibility of the resources transferred under programme support, it is important to ensure that this form of co-operation takes place, as appropriate, in the context of a reform programme agreed with the IMF and the World Bank. While recognising the special role of these institutions in providing funding and advice for economic reform, bilateral agencies should be vigilant in maintaining the prominence of poverty reduction objectives in the design of any reform programme. In this regard, programme support can open the way to a continuing dialogue on pro-poor policies in the critical areas of macroeconomic reform and good governance.

### Sector support

In pursuit of effective development co-operation, many donors view sector support, in the form of Sector-Wide Approaches (SWAps), as a potentially strong instrument for enhancing local ownership, strengthening partnership, co-ordinating external and domestic resources, and establishing a conducive institutional environment for development and poverty reduction.

**New approaches to sector support hold potential for fostering ownership and participation by stakeholders at all levels...**

The Sector-Wide Approach is a mechanism for agencies and their partner countries to support the integrated development of a sector. Agencies make their contributions towards a single sector policy and expenditure programme, under government leadership, striving to use as far as possible common management and reporting procedures to disburse and account for all funds. SWAps are fairly recent and still wrestling with the complexity of institutional reform and stakeholder involvement. They may become a promising way to implement partnership strategies for reducing poverty provided that existing constraints are overcome by strengthening the necessary institutional capacities, facilitating planning and implementation both at the national and local levels and fostering stakeholders' ownership in sector programmes.

Sector programmes imply a different approach to aid management from what development agencies are used to and organised for. It requires development agencies to fully take into account locally-owned sector strategies. And it calls for greater modesty and an acceptance of what may be a slow process of change, relying on partnership-building rather than on the implementation of a blueprint. Extending this form of support greatly depends on the country context and is premised on a number of prerequisites, including the ability of the partner country to fulfil the responsibilities of adequate financial governance.

So far, the new approaches to sector support are still in the formative stages. To realise the distinct advantages of sector programmes for aid effectiveness and poverty reduction, limited experience points to the following challenges which agencies committed to this kind of support should address.

**Focus on the poverty reduction objective.** Sector programmes are a good mechanism for discussing resource allocation and how equity and effectiveness relate to poverty reduction. Policy dialogue on the rights of the poor and gender issues in specific sectors can influence political and administrative processes to be more responsive to poor people's needs and demands. Sector funding also has the considerable benefit of internalising issues that are part of the environment of projects (for example excessive expenditure on regional hospitals at the expense of primary health care). But even in the social sectors, it is often not easy to reconcile sector approaches with a strong focus on reducing poverty *per se*. Deliberate steps may be necessary to ensure that progress is made, not only in producing better services, but also in facilitating access to them and improving the well-being of the poor. It may be necessary to devise targeting mechanisms that disproportionately concentrate services on poor areas, disadvantaged communities and vulnerable groups.

**... and for focusing on poor peoples' needs.**

**Sector support requires a strong emphasis on building capacities...**

**Emphasise capacity-building components.** The sector approach presupposes a more active role for all levels of government in co-ordinating agencies, formulating policies, setting priorities and implementing programmes. The implementation of sector programmes requires substantial institutional reforms, including the need to redefine roles within the political-administrative hierarchy and to determine how responsibilities can be shared among public, private and community sectors. There are capacity constraints for such complex programmes in the public sector and among private and civil society actors, creating major bottlenecks in sector policy design and throughout programme implementation and monitoring. This underscores the need, in the preparatory phases of sector programmes, to add and to integrate capacity-building and participation components. This is essential for securing a well-grounded policy to which most stakeholders have contributed and which they have the capacity to implement.

**... involving local government...**

**Facilitate co-ordination with local government.** National governments may be assuming increased responsibility for sector programmes, but this does not necessarily mean greater ownership by stakeholders below the national level or outside the public sector. Because sector programming is the responsibility of the central authority and its line ministries, local government, which tends to take a more multisectoral approach to resource allocation and to be more responsive to local needs, may lose influence. Development agencies should support analyses which explore the best balance between national and local responsibility and the requirements for improving co-ordination between different levels of administration. This is particularly important in the context of decentralisation, which aims to empower local government authorities. Technical co-operation agents who are an integral part of sector programmes can act as experts in supporting participation at all levels and mediation among different interest groups, thus becoming catalysts for results on the ground.

**... and forging public-private partnerships.**

**Foster public-private partnerships.** Involving civil society in sector programmes is a major challenge. In such productive sectors as agriculture and infrastructure, privatisation features prominently, but sector programmes tend to be seen as public sector programmes. It is important, therefore, to keep in mind the principle of building on the combined and complementary action of all the stakeholders involved. In such social sectors as health and education, the regulatory roles of line ministries can be strengthened while the decentralised management of service delivery can be encouraged, giving a stronger role to private providers of services (community-based organisations, NGOs and the private sector).

**Seek synergies with other sector policies.** A major rationale behind sector programmes is to overcome the fragmentation of unco-ordinated investments, particularly donor-supported (and often donor-managed) projects, by bringing together all sector activities within a common framework. This is leading to considerable progress in co-ordination around country-owned sector strategies. But concentrating on a single sector may also mean that opportunities for co-ordination and synergies with other sector policies may be missed. This is particularly important in relation to reducing poverty since poor people do not live in sectors. Poverty cuts across sectors and needs to be tackled accordingly. This is a real challenge given that co-ordination among line ministries is extremely complex, disrupting ingrained routines and taxing the limited institutional capacity of the different bureaucracies.

Good practice makes concern for the poor an explicit priority in all sector programmes. In this connection, it is important to rely on poverty assessments (see Part 1) that embrace both quantitative and qualitative data, disaggregated by gender, age, social categories and covering geographical, cultural and socio-economic dimensions. In this way, the multidimensional nature of poverty and its contributing factors can form the basis of sector programmes and provide essential links to a country's strategy for reducing poverty.

**Harmonise accounting and reporting procedures.** Funding for sector support may use parallel financing mechanisms (budget lines) or may be deposited in a common basket. It is subject to agreement between the partners on certain broad principles governing the use of the sector budget. Ultimately, development agencies will have to identify practices to ease the burden on their partners who have to comply with a multiplicity of differing and complex donor procedures. Major efforts are needed to achieve a degree of simplification and, to the extent possible, harmonisation in procedures, bearing in mind the need to ensure transparency and accountability. In this regard the DAC Task Force on Donor Practices is expected to provide further guidance aimed at strengthening ownership and at reducing the transaction costs and accountability risks involved in delivering aid for both the development agency and the partner country. On the government side, this will require developing transparent systems for budgeting and independent expenditure control and auditing.

*Funding for sector support calls for greater harmonisation of agency reporting procedures matched by increased transparency and accountability in partner countries.*

To sum up, the multiple concerns with building institutional capacity, involving local government, forging public-private partnerships, and strengthening ownership and accountability may initially divert attention from the primary objective of reducing poverty. But experience shows that this can be overcome in second-generation programmes, where the potential of sector programmes to reduce poverty is more likely to be realised. Involvement of experienced agency staff in the field is crucial for carrying out the policy dialogue on poverty reduction and to help address these challenges.

Emphasis on sector support is leading to a more focused dialogue on social development policies and programmes, particularly in the health and education sectors so essential to poverty reduction (Boxes 10 and 11).

### Area-based approaches

Despite an historical legacy of inefficiency, integrated approaches limited to a specific rural area have recently re-emerged in the context of political and economic liberalisation in partner countries. Where local authorities have sufficient autonomy and where rural markets are liberalised, it becomes possible to operate without the top-down institutional framework that contributed to the failure of the former Integrated Rural Development Programmes. Behind the renewal of interest in area-based approaches is also the desire of agencies to tackle the multidimensionality of poverty and to focus on sustainable livelihoods[2] by cutting across sectors.

*A new generation of area-based approaches aim at adressing the multiple dimensions of poverty.*

Often focused on rural production (crops, livestock, fishery, forestry, conservation), area-based approaches support such basic services as health, education and water supply as well as infrastructure (for example rural roads) and small-scale off-farm employment. The starting point is to take a holistic approach and consider the diversity of factors that affect the income and well-being of the poor. This assumes a good understanding of the social, institutional and policy contexts of poor people's livelihood, including the dynamics of gender relations and the use of participatory approaches to gather information. Many programmes focus on building capacities in both communities and local administrations, in some cases creating space for participatory negotiation where the voices of poor people or their representatives can be heard.

## Box 10. Sector support for dealing with poverty: education in Uganda

The Ugandan Universal Primary Education programme is a good example of a sector-wide approach for education. It draws together the key elements of a partnership focused on reducing poverty.

The programme was initiated by strong leadership from a Head of State committed to universal primary education.

Policy was developed in a broadly participatory process, which included some consultation with groups in civil society and, at a later stage, representatives of the poor.

Budget allocations to the sector – which increased and were protected as part of the Poverty Action Fund – reflected high-level political commitment.

The design of the programme was directly informed by in-depth poverty analysis, based on household surveys and participatory poverty assessments, which fed into expenditure priorities through the medium-term fiscal framework.

Government ownership of this initiative attracted strong support from development agencies that shared the priority given to primary education.

The programme also provides a model of good practice in strengthening accountability in implementation. Key features include:

- Locating the analysis of poverty and monitoring within the powerful Ministry of Finance.

- Involving parliament, civil society and development agencies in policy decisions and monitoring programme implementation.

- Insisting on transparency to enable users of the education services to hold providers accountable through multiple sources of information and channels for providing suggestions for improvement.

- Actions to deal with the diversion of resources (directed to schools but absorbed by districts).

- Efforts to empower communities by inviting their representatives to sit on school committees and giving them some financial responsibility.

Provided that they are partner-country-driven and kept financially and institutionally sustainable, the new area-based approaches can help to create an enabling local environment for reducing poverty. But they raise the recurrent problem of scale and sustainability so long as these efforts are limited to externally-supported project areas. The relationship with government and compliance with national priorities will need to be carefully reviewed to avoid the sort of enclave development that prevailed in the past. Fundamentally, reforms to place local government on a secure and democratic basis are key to the long-term success in area-based anti-poverty work. This issue involves the broader question of decentralisation, including the devolution of responsibility and funding for basic service delivery and its relevance to poverty reduction.

### Project support

**To be sustainable projects should be embedded in national planning frameworks or sector-wide approaches.**

Projects have a long history as instruments of development co-operation. They have the advantage of being able to select a manageable set of problems from a complex and confusing reality and prescribe the inputs needed to foster local development. But experience in many agencies shows that free-standing projects have serious limitations in the contexts of specific partner countries. If they are not included in the national planning frameworks, they can distort the pattern of national spending by using separate funding channels and may impose high management costs. These isolated projects are often characterised by top-down donor management in both design and implementation phases, with resulting problems of sustainability after the withdrawal of external funding.

## Box 11.  Promoting pro-poor health systems

Good health is vital to reducing poverty and promoting social and economic development. Indeed, recent analyses of the causes of growth have called attention to the role of better health and lower population growth. So, three of the Millennium Development Goals for 2015 focus on health outcomes: reducing infant and child mortality by two-thirds, reducing maternal mortality by three-quarters, halting and reversing the spread of HIV/AIDS and the incidence of malaria and other major diseases.

To realise these goals it is essential to give priority to the health of the poor, because it is their key asset for surviving and making a living. The following have been identified as good practices for enhancing the poverty focus of health systems:

■ **Mobilise commitment, partnerships and resources for pro-poor health.** Bring health to the centre of the dialogue on strategies for reducing poverty. Identify policies outside the health sector that can improve health. Expand partnership to involve civil society and the private sector (as in the eradication of polio). Increase the very low level of aid to health (about 6% of ODA) in support of country-owned, poverty-focused programmes in the health sector in line with the 20/20 target.

■ **Make health systems more responsive to the needs of poor people.** Provide quality health services. Establish affordable and equitable payment systems. Train health staff to respect the dignity of poor people. Address the causes of deprivation: gender discrimination, social exclusion, geographical isolation.

■ **Focus on the health threats perpetuating poverty.** Shift attention to major diseases – malaria, diarrhoea, tuberculosis – that are prevalent among the poor. Address maternal morbidity and mortality, the AIDS pandemic, tobacco and environmentally-related diseases. Health risks need to be assessed locally as well as nationally and the specific risks faced by men, women and children should be highlighted. Disaggregated health data by income, age, sex and locality should be complemented by participatory research that documents the health needs expressed by the poor.

In addition, international action can stimulate the development of global public goods in health (for example, through a focus on poverty-related diseases and their vaccines).

For these reasons, development agencies are moving to project modalities that have the potential for more sustained outcomes and greater effects on poverty. The emphasis now is on designing activities within a broader development framework as part of national-level support or sector-wide approaches. Empowerment projects are emerging that stress ownership, participation and sustainability. They aim to increase local capacities and empower communities to organise and mobilise themselves. They also promote leadership by stakeholders in planning and implementation and in laying the foundations for financial sustainability. Two fundamental factors for success are the compatibility of the project with the surrounding institutional and cultural framework and its acceptance by local and central public authorities and by civil society.

Good practice in reducing poverty calls for projects that address the multiple concerns of the poor (for example income, dignity and security) while encouraging and strengthening their abilities and capacities to achieve sustainable livelihoods. This includes:

■ Identifying the poor and their condition through poverty assessments and beneficiary needs assessments.

■ Drawing on poor people's knowledge of their situation, their actions and their coping strategies using participatory approaches to involve them in projects.

■ Elevating gender to a primary rather than a secondary concern throughout the project cycle.

## Box 12. Ensuring a poverty focus in infrastructure projects

To ensure that projects focus on reducing poverty, they should be screened for each of the following elements: technique, area, focus and organisation. What follows comes from investment projects in infrastructure where links with poverty reduction may not be as obvious as in the case of social projects.

■ **Technique:** Labour-intensive methods are often more pro-poor than equipment-based approaches. In road construction, labour-based methods are often cheaper and create important links to the local economy. But care must be taken to give women access to these jobs, as recruitment may create gender-based constraints.

■ **Area:** Support should be directed to areas or regions where the poor predominate. For instance, rural electrification is more pro-poor than urban electrification, and infrastructure improvements in slums are more poverty-focused than general urban development. But there are trade-offs: capital investment decisions on the most efficient use of resources may favour infrastructure choices that stimulate rapid and broad-based development. For instance, there may be strong demand for energy from an emerging private sector with the ability to generate employment and tax revenues, but not located in regions where the poor live.

■ **Focus:** Secondary and feeder roads are often more important to the poor than primary roads. To access markets, the rural poor typically need better roads and more frequent transportation opportunities. Since the rural poor are often spatially scattered, a fine-meshed net of secondary roads is more important than high-quality inter-city transportation, which is not of great concern to the urban poor. In some situations, financing recurrent costs may be more important to the poor than the initial investments. However, agencies are often unable to secure government commitment to cover the recurrent costs of operating and maintaining the infrastructure projects they support.

■ **Organisation:** In supporting infrastructure it is important to identify and to take into account local needs and priorities. While infrastructure improvements have often been approached from a national, technical perspective, it is widely acknowledged that the participation of poor communities substantially influences the long-term functioning and sustainability of infrastructure. Considering the opinions of poor people on infrastructure programmes may also increase their effect on poverty.

## Poverty-focused support and targeted interventions

**Targeted interventions aim at mobilising poor communities through participation, self-help and empowerment.**

Targeting poor people is a way of ensuring that projects focus on the actions and strategies of the poor (the landless, slum-dwellers, female-headed households). Development agencies provide targeted support through such instruments as integrated food security programmes and food-for-work programmes, social funds and micro-finance. These micro-level interventions aim at helping poor communities to reduce their vulnerability to risk (whether structural because of chronic poverty, or transitory because of short-term shocks). They generally put a premium on grassroots mobilisation, participation, self-help and empowerment.

**Food-for-work programmes** are targeted interventions that appeal primarily to poor people: they tend not to attract the better-off because they provide low levels of benefit. The record is mixed on the sustainability of their impact on poverty.

**Social funds** are grants from development agencies for small projects managed by poor communities. They seek to empower the poor by actively engaging them in identifying development priorities (primarily in health, education and water supply), managing project funds and maintaining facilities and services beyond project completion. Experience with social funds is mixed – they are difficult to sustain and problematic when used to promote local political goals rather than concentrating on reducing poverty. They may bypass previously agreed budget priorities within a given sector (by, say, supporting the establishment of new health centres not in line with the national health sector programme). Experience is positive where the funds have a clear mandate to reduce poverty, to concentrate on local activities and to complement government-initiated activities without distorting established priorities.

**Micro-finance** schemes are often designed to reduce the vulnerability of poor households by widening their income-generating options, increasing their productivity and empowering women. But micro-finance schemes often fail to reach those living in extreme poverty and, alone, rarely increase incomes enough to raise people out of poverty. They have greater impact when combined with assistance to develop business and marketing skills, to identify markets for locally-produced goods and to purchase and use land in the best way. Plans to improve access to finance for the poor must also consider gender differences. This means overcoming the collateral issue when legal or cultural barriers prevent women from holding land title or other assets. It also means providing information on how to access and use credit, especially for women who may be excluded from beneficiary groups or who lack the time to apply. Micro-finance schemes will have limited impact if not backed by macro-policies that support financial markets and facilitate the spread of viable informal financial institutions. In rural areas, most public credit systems are not organised to serve the poor, and private sector banking institutions, which increasingly replace them, do not consider the poor to be good credit risks or a profitable market. Thus, special credit service strategies are needed to reach the poor.

In supporting small projects or targeted interventions, development agencies should be careful to ensure that highly visible operations focused on limited numbers of poor people do not divert attention from equally important indirect and sector-wide programmes that affect larger numbers of poor people.

## Technical co-operation for capacity development

Technical co-operation (TC) is often a major component of the development co-operation instruments described above. It has a continuing and fundamental role to play in underpinning the formulation of poverty reduction strategies and the implementation of pro-poor programmes. Whether free-standing or combined with financial co-operation to support specific programmes, sectors or projects, technical co-operation aims to strengthen institutional and human capacities in partner countries. By improving legal and administrative frameworks, human resources efficiency and the functioning of organisations, TC is also key to making development co-operation more effective.

*Capacity development should be given the highest priority when supporting partners' efforts to formulate and implement poverty reduction strategies.*

Capacity development should be given highest priority when supporting partners' efforts to create a more conducive environment for poverty reduction. Many partner countries require functioning institutions and skilled human capacity in the public, private and non-governmental sectors in order to carry forward and sustain reform programmes in the broad areas of macroeconomic policies, good governance and social development so critical to reducing poverty. Development agencies can strengthen national and local capacities for policy-making, for planning and managing sector programmes and for delivering improved social services in terms of quality, equity, access and efficiency. In addition, technical co-operation agents can act as facilitators in moderating multi-stakeholders processes. Mediation is particularly important in the context of poverty reduction where conflicts of interests between different groups of society are bound to arise.

Capacity development initiatives must also take into account the strong advance of the AIDS pandemic in many poor countries. AIDS hits the poor hardest – by decimating national administrative capacity for poverty reduction, by depriving poor households of their breadwinners and by increasing the number of orphan-headed households. Relying on more participatory processes to build consensus around poverty reduction strategies also calls for improving the capacities of civil society to participate more effectively in policy formulation and implementation. It also requires building the capacities of advocacy groups that help poor people gain influence as a political constituency.

**The long-term impact of development co-operation depends on applying a range of well-tested approaches.**

The success of technical co-operation, within the context of country ownership, depends strongly on development agency commitment to apply well-tested approaches for upgrading the effectiveness and long-term impact of TC programmes.[2] These include the following:

- Setting self-reliance as a strategic objective by focusing on long-term capacity-building, rather than achieving short-term performance improvements by filling gaps in competence.

- Planning technical co-operation activities in the context of partner country poverty reduction strategies and sector programmes, instead of making isolated supply-driven TC proposals.

- Defining objectives in terms of outcomes to be achieved, rather than inputs to be provided.

- Encouraging greater use of local expertise and defining specific roles for international experts where needed.

- Building on existing institutions and capacity, both public and private, rather than promoting parallel structures.

- Using participatory planning and management tools and building on political change processes that are home-grown.

- Assessing the capacity of partner countries to meet recurrent costs and to include TC-related expenditure in the national budget.

High priority should be given to technical co-operation activities that are likely to have broad impacts by helping the poor to improve their access to basic social services (education, health) and – for women and other socially marginalised groups engaged in small farming and micro-enterprises – by facilitating their access to credit, technology and advice. Moving towards greater decentralisation also implies a renewed role for technical co-operation in strengthening local governments, municipalities and such private institutions as local credit institutions and professional associations. To meet future challenges in reducing poverty, TC will also play a crucial role in strengthening good governance, democratic processes, protection of human rights, respect for the rule of law as well as markets and private sector development.

## Special focus instruments

This section provides guidance on the use of debt relief, humanitarian assistance and support for regional co-operation, three areas of rising importance in agency portfolios and which have significant linkages to poverty reduction.

### Debt relief

**Debt relief is an integral part of the international community's contribution to reducing poverty.**

In heavily indebted poor countries (HIPCs), debt service payments in hard currency drain scarce domestic resources from investments in such areas as education and health, which are central to reducing poverty. Debt relief is therefore an integral part of the international community's contribution to poverty reduction. Various mechanisms are being used from outright forgiveness to debt for nature swaps and the conversion of bilateral debt to fund local grant-giving foundations.

Through the enhanced HIPC initiative, OECD Member governments pledge to provide broader and faster debt relief with the specific objective of releasing funds for reducing poverty. The poverty-reducing impact of this unprecedented effort depends, on the one hand, on progress made by HIPCs in developing and implementing strategies for poverty reduction and, on the other hand, on OECD countries securing the required financing without reducing other aid flows. To ensure that the funds released by debt relief are properly used, monitoring systems should be set up to screen budget expenditure.

In the future, steps will have to be taken by lenders and borrowing countries to avoid further accumulation of unsustainable debt. As a complement to the HIPC debt cancellations, development agencies should explore other opportunities for debt relief. These may include conversion of debt into capacity-building programmes in areas where they are likely to have a strong impact on reducing poverty. At the same time it is important not to lose sight of the assistance needs of countries with good policies that have avoided serious debt problems.

### Assistance for conflict prevention and humanitarian aid

In helping to prevent violent conflict and restore peace, development co-operation should focus on addressing poverty and inequality as both causes and consequences of conflict. Simultaneously, it should give long-term support to strengthen governance and to build appropriate institutions and democratic mechanisms for resolving tensions without violence. When acute emergencies, violent conflict or natural disasters arise, humanitarian assistance provides a quick response, often on a large scale, concentrated on saving lives and relieving suffering.

**Development co-operation should focus on addressing poverty and inequality as both causes and consequences of conflict.**

Since poor people often lack the means to avoid crises, such assistance is, by definition, poverty-focused. But it may undermine poverty reduction by creating dependencies and impeding the problem-solving and self-governing abilities of afflicted communities. Good practice in this respect includes planning such assistance so that it:

- Integrates the long-term needs of beneficiaries and the coping strategies of the poor.

- Incorporates gender analyses as standard practice.

- Does not undermine local production and service delivery by flooding local markets with foodstuffs.

- Supports local capacities for taking over the management of relief operations as soon as possible.[4]

A major challenge for humanitarian assistance is to integrate relief and rehabilitation into the context of longer-term approaches aimed at fostering self-reliance.

### Support for regional co-operation

Formulating a country strategy for poverty reduction requires a regional as well as a national vision. In many partner countries, regional perspectives and solutions are necessary to compensate for national limitations related to small market size or poor resource endowments. Regional markets provide opportunities for increased growth by improving competitiveness and productivity, so they are important as a stepping stone for facilitating integration into the global economy. Regional co-operation can facilitate greater co-ordination of economic reform policies and harmonised regulatory frameworks, essential for expanding investment opportunities and spurring growth. The benefits of greater regional integration have started to show – intra-regional trade within Asia, Africa and Latin America has intensified in the 1990s and increased much more rapidly than trade with OECD countries.

**Formulating a country strategy for poverty reduction requires a regional as well as a national vision.**

Coping strategies of the poor are often regional in scope, involving migration as one or more family members move to neighbouring countries to broaden income-earning opportunities. These migrants provide an important source of income for their families through workers' remittances and bring home new ideas and skills that, in turn, contribute to income-generating activities.

At the same time solutions will have to be found for regional issues that impact on poverty. For instance, the productivity of labour and the livelihoods of poor households are seriously affected by cross-border diseases such as AIDS, or by the degradation of shared natural resources such as river basin and watershed systems, soil erosion and desertification.

Development agencies should integrate regional dimensions of poverty reduction in their country strategies. In particular, they should consider how the poverty reduction strategies of partner countries could benefit from regional institutions, capacities and markets. Centres of excellence in some sub-regions can help lower the costs of training and research with important economies of scale. Such regional centres and professional networks can play important roles in the country-led analyses of poverty that inform strategy and policy options. They can also contribute to evaluating the results of poverty reduction while enhancing national capacity to implement poverty reduction strategies.

## Conclusion

### Poverty reduction should be at the centre of policy dialogue and the starting point for planning and implementing development co-operation.

Where there is political support in partner countries, pro-poor development co-operation should assess the following elements:

- The capacity to understand and link poverty to governance and to economic and social policy – particularly in the cases of gender and other institutional systems that shape entitlements.

- The allocation of resources to the poor by sectors and the access to and quality of public services. This calls for creating sufficient room in national budgets through the best use of domestic resources and of debt relief.

- Political commitment and the willingness within the administrative system to implement the proposed reforms and monitor outcomes.

# Notes

1. See *DAC Strategies for Sustainable Development: Guidance for Development Co-operation Agencies* (2001).

2. For a definition of sustainable livelihood, see Part 1, "Which policy actions are required?", (f).

3. See "DAC Principles for New Orientations in Technical Co-operation", in *DAC Principles for Effective Aid*, OECD, Paris, 1992.

4. See the *DAC Guidelines on Conflict, Peace and Development Co-operation* (1998), and *Helping Prevent Violent Conflit: Orientations for External Partners*.

# 4 Towards policy coherence for poverty reduction

## Introduction

The preceding parts of these *Guidelines* have made clear that for development co-operation policies to be effective, they must be fully consistent with, and focused on, the objective of reducing poverty in partner countries. But at least as important is the degree of overall coherence between the policies of OECD Member governments with regard to their impact on global poverty reduction.

*The co-ordination, consistency and coherence of all policies affecting global poverty are essential...*

To distinguish between the closely related concepts of policy coherence, consistency and co-ordination, definitions are provided in Box 13.

Policy coherence for poverty reduction is a major challenge because the specific issues commonly involve domestic interest groups and government agencies with primary interests and responsibilities other than that of reducing global poverty. There may be conflict, for example, between a government's efforts to meet the concerns of particular interests or communities and its commitment to reduce poverty in developing countries. The degree of policy consistency tends to diminish with the domestic political sensitivity of such policy issues and associated interests, and increases when there is a strong domestic constituency for efforts to alleviate and eliminate poverty in poor countries.

Policy co-ordination is required to address conflicting interests and objectives, which are reinforced by the compartmentalisation of politics and public administration. Policy co-ordination is thus a political as well as an administrative process. Development agencies are often in a fairly weak position politically compared with most other government departments and public and private interests associated with areas such as trade, investment, agriculture and national security. However, there are a number of reasons why poverty reduction might now receive more weight in relation to other national objectives, and become a higher priority for a broader range of policy-makers:

*... and harmonising these with other policy objectives having strong domestic political support is a major challenge...*

- World leaders and institutions such as the G7/8, the IMF, the World Bank, the OECD and the UN have adopted policy statements which make poverty reduction a common frame of reference and a major objective of policy.

- Poverty is increasingly recognised as a "global public bad", not only on moral grounds, but also as a source of dysfunction and disorder in the world, with adverse spillover effects in the form of political instability, environmental degradation, migration flows, etc.

- Awareness that the OECD population is now just 1 billion out of a world total of 6 billion is increasing. This trend will be exacerbated by the pressures of population growth: 97% of the estimated increase of 2 billion people over the next twenty years will live in the developing world. Thus, global well-being depends increasingly on solving the development problems of poor countries.

*... but poverty reduction is increasingly becoming a high priority for leaders and policy-makers, for several reasons,...*

---

### Box 13. The dimensions of policy coherence

The coherence challenge has a number of dimensions that need to be addressed in a synchronised manner, while recognising that full coherence is never a realistic outcome.

■ *Policy co-ordination* means getting the various institutional and managerial systems, which formulate policy, to work together.

■ *Policy consistency* means ensuring that individual policies are not internally contradictory, and avoiding policies that

conflict with reaching for a given policy objective, in this case international poverty reduction.

■ *Policy coherence* goes further; it involves the systematic promotion of mutually reinforcing policy actions across government departments and agencies creating synergies towards achieving the defined objective.

---

**...... which facilitates enhanced policy coherence with immense potential impact on poverty reduction.**

Improving policy coherence in OECD countries could be of major significance for developing countries. Estimates by the Secretariats of the OECD and the World Bank indicate that OECD tariffs and subsidies for agriculture and manufactured goods may cause annual losses to the developing countries in the same order of magnitude as their total ODA receipts. If the impact of non-tariff barriers, protection of services and other relevant trade policy measures causing transfer and transaction costs is added, the total static cost of OECD protection on developing countries may be over three times the amount of ODA, and the dynamic effects even larger. The cost to OECD countries of implementing agricultural policies alone amount to about $1 billion per day, which is nearly seven times the level of ODA expenditures by DAC Member countries.

For the Millennium Development Goals to be achieved, it is crucial that Members make further progress to ensure policy coherence. In adopting the strategic policy document *Shaping the 21st Century,* the DAC stated that "we should aim for nothing less than to assure that the entire range of relevant industrialised country policies are consistent with and do not undermine development objectives".

## Globalisation and policy coherence

**Globalisation has led to greater interdependance and market integration...**

Policy coherence has to be looked at in the overall context of the process of globalisation. Rapid growth in the movement of people, goods, services, capital, technology and information across national borders is creating an increasingly integrated global economy. This is the core meaning of globalisation, and it has led to a world that is more interconnected and interdependent than ever before. This increasing openness and integration of the world economy is creating conditions that could make possible a massive reduction in poverty across the world. Globalisation is creating huge wealth and has the potential to generate benefits for all. However, this will only happen with purposeful policy action by the international community and by governments.

**... through rapid economic and technological changes that create huge opportunities for wealth creation...**

Fast changing information and communications technologies (ICTs) are transforming markets, including financial markets, and require new methods of organising work, business and trade to harness the benefits of globalisation. At the same time, many people are seriously concerned about the rapid economic and technological changes now under way. The importance of addressing these concerns locally, nationally and internationally has been recognised by OECD Ministers.

Globalisation presents new opportunities as well as new challenges to all countries, regions, societies and people. While world exports of goods and services have grown at unprecedented and sustained rates since the early 1980s, the share of developing countries (78% of the world's population) is only 18%. Despite their preferential market access, the share of the least developed countries (LDC, 11% of world population) fell to 0.5% in 1999.

---

### Box 14. An illustrative checklist on policy coherence for poverty reduction

In the year 2000, the OECD Ministerial Council and the DAC High Level Meeting decided to develop a checklist for policy coherence that could be a reference point for public policies in Member countries. A checklist is included in the *Guidelines* (see Annex). It covers a range of issues that impact on development. The checklist is illustrative rather than definitive, and serves to encourage Member governments systematically to integrate development and poverty issues into all relevant policy areas. It has been elaborated after consultations with a wide range of policy experts in the OECD. It is designed as a compact standalone reference document to be used by different policy communities in Member governments, and also to promote and guide further work within the OECD itself on policy coherence issues.

---

The poorest countries are not in a position to secure significant benefits from increased trade opportunities without special measures to support economic and social development and institutional capacity-building. Similarly, poorer regions and groups in all countries are at a disadvantage in the increasingly competitive world of economic and technological globalisation.

In the context of poverty reduction, the key challenge is to ensure that developing countries, and especially poor people in those countries, benefit from globalisation and are able to adapt successfully to this new environment. Towards this end, it is critical to secure the commitment and participation of developing countries in the international systems and frameworks of co-operation that govern a wide range of social and economic policies. This means giving weight to their concerns and perspectives, and supporting their capacity to act as fully-fledged partners in international negotiations in development-relevant policy areas.

**... but also concerns; the key challenge is how to ensure that the poor benefit in an increasingly competitive world economy...**

The lead responsibility for addressing this challenge rests with the governments of developing countries. However, greater policy coherence between OECD government policies is essential for enabling developing countries to take advantage of the processes of globalisation and to reduce poverty. Globalisation requires OECD governments, more than ever before, to take account of the broader development objectives in all policies and external relationships.

In a world where there is no longer a clear distinction between domestic and international affairs, effective development co-operation programmes alone will not adequately reduce poverty. Development objectives need to be integrated throughout the full range of government departments, not only in developing countries but also in OECD countries. How this can be done and the lessons of experience are the topics of the following sections. The focus areas for enhanced policy coherence are presented in the last main section and summarised in Box 16. An extended list is included in the illustrative checklist in the Annex.

**... through enhanced policy coherence towards that end across international organisations and governments in developing as well as OECD countries.**

## How can policy coherence be enhanced?

Progress towards policy coherence requires a knowledge of the mechanisms that link various policies to poverty in developing countries. Substantial evidence is now available that indicates how policies in a number of areas may impede the reduction of poverty.

The role of each policy, its impact on poverty and where, within government, it can be adjusted for enhanced coherence call for careful analysis. This requires adequate resources for policy analysis. The results should form part of the brief to policy-makers engaged in inter-ministerial co-ordination and in international negotiations. Coherence may never be perfect, but there are areas where much can be achieved with relatively little effort.

**Policy coherence requires sound, evidence-based policy analysis of poverty links and impacts...**

**... as a basis for policy co-ordination and political negotiations involving civil society;...**

**... it includes integrating gender perspectives in the policy formulation process...**

Policy adjustment in pursuit of greater coherence is likely to be part of a political process. It is important that the different policy-makers and stakeholders have the knowledge necessary to make the case for this adjustment. In this respect, NGOs and the media can play a major role in informing the public, but it is important that the information they have be reliable and based on facts and sound analysis.

Gender-related differences in economic opportunity are often exacerbated by incoherent policies. For example, many of the producers and consumers most affected by opening up an economy to globalisation are women. Their situation regarding access to the resources, information and technology required to seize the opportunities afforded by globalisation is critical. Gender analysis is therefore central to both policy formulation and the assessment of policy impact. It can also contribute both to an understanding of poverty and to the development of effective policies and initiatives. Adopting a gender perspective from the outset of the process of policy formation will help to ensure that positive outcomes are enhanced, and negative outcomes avoided or mitigated.

**... and fully-fledged participation of developing countries in international forums...**

Policy coherence should lead OECD governments to promote and support the participation of developing countries in various international forums, such as the World Trade Organisation, the Financial Stability Forum, and the Food Aid Convention. Not only should the formal sessions of these forums be open to developing nations, but so, too, should those informal meetings that are so important to the outcome of negotiations. Policy coherence will also require transparency and accountability in these deliberations, including those of the international financial institutions.

**... with support from DAC Members, including for capacity-building.**

The capacity of developing countries to participate in negotiating and implementing international agreements, and their capacity to reap the benefits from them, need substantial strengthening. Several DAC Members offer programmes for capacity-building related to international trade – both in negotiating skills for civil servants and for developing the private sector's ability to compete in the global economy. The successful promotion of the ability of developing countries to export may increase the competition of firms in OECD countries. Important tests for policy coherence arise if and when exports from developing countries encounter entrenched protectionist interests in potential markets.

# Lessons from experience in OECD countries

Several OECD governments have extensive experience in trying to enhance policy coherence with respect to poverty reduction. A review of this experience suggests several important conclusions. A major conclusion is that coherent policies substantially enhance the effectiveness of efforts to reduce poverty. Coherence also promotes the credibility and legitimacy of OECD governments *vis-à-vis* their partners.

Summit meetings such as the UN Millennium Assembly and the annual G-8 meetings have demonstrated the importance of sending the message of poverty reduction from the top. Once it is enunciated clearly, channels for forging coherent policies in relation to the centrifugal forces of sector and special interests are much more easily strengthened.

Policy coherence calls for effective consultation with public agencies and private stakeholders. It has proven helpful to appoint an authoritative policy co-ordination unit, preferably high in the executive branch of government, to establish strong links across a wide range of government ministries and agencies and with civil society. Formal contact sessions are an invaluable tool for improving coherence, but providing a suitable organisational culture for informal contact is also critical.

A clear official statement from the government that its goal is to reduce poverty enhances policy coherence. For example, within the last few years, the *United Kingdom* has published two White Papers on Eliminating World Poverty in which the principles for partnership and for consistent policies concerning a wide range of policy areas are clearly stated. Formal procedures have been instituted to ensure the intra-government linkages required for policy coherence. In addition, cabinet status has been granted to the Secretary for International Development, increasing the status of poverty reduction as a national objective (see Box 15).

The *United States* is increasingly using inter-agency working groups to set international policies and to discuss issues of policy coherence and trade-offs. In this context, efforts are made to reach a consensual decision that recognises development concerns. Examples are wide-ranging and include the Committee on International Science, Engineering and Technology, which makes policy recommendations to the Executive; the Inter-Agency Working Group on HIPCs led by the Treasury department, which has adopted poverty reduction concerns as an integral part of its HIPC mandate and the Enterprise for the Americas Foundation, which converts debt into local development grants and is co-governed by the departments of Treasury, State and USAID.

In the *Netherlands*, the Ministry of Foreign Affairs (MFA) is in charge of all aspects of relations between the Netherlands and developing countries. The aim of this "de-compartmentalisation" is to create synergies within and across all parts of the Dutch government, thus improving overall policy coherence and effectiveness. The Bilateral Department of the MFA integrates development co-operation with other aspects of foreign policy and trade relations. The Council for European and International Affairs, a committee established by the cabinet, is in charge of overseeing policy coherence.

*Switzerland's* North-South Guidelines place particular emphasis on the need for coherence between the various policies that have an impact on developing countries. They have contributed to an increased awareness of policy coherence problems. Formal consultation procedures, involving both offices and ministries, aim at ensuring that inconsistencies are identified and, as far as possible, resolved. A consultative commission, comprising representatives from a broad cross-section of civil society, advises the government on development co-operation and is also an institutional tool for enhancing policy coherence. NGOs and political organisations are regularly consulted.

**Policy coherence in OECD countries increases effectiveness of efforts to reduce poverty and promotes credibility vis-à-vis partner countries...**

**... especially when the message is signalled from the top...**

**... and backed by consultations with public agencies and private stakeholders through a central policy co-ordination unit and informal contacts.**

**OECD Members are doing this in many different ways.**

---

## Box 15. Promoting policy coherence in the United Kingdom

The UK has taken far-reaching initiatives in promoting policy coherence. The main elements are:

■ The Government has made a clear political commitment. The Department for International Development (DFID) was established as a separate department within the Government, and its Secretary given full cabinet status. Following extensive discussions between government departments, a White Paper was elaborated, presented to Parliament and widely publicised.

■ Resources were committed to policy coherence. DFID's capacity to analyse the implications for the development of trade and investment issues and to engage in a process of debate within the Government was strengthened. DFID also commissioned research related to the liberalisation of agricultural trade, food security and biodiversity.

■ Mechanisms for policy co-ordination between government departments were strengthened. At the Ministerial level, an Inter-departmental Working Group on Development was created to deal with cross-cutting issues. DFID was represented on an official group, chaired by the Department of Trade and Industry, which met regularly to discuss the UK's approach to multilateral trade negotiations.

■ DFID's links were strengthened with multilateral organisations such as WTO, UNCTAD, ITC, and the World Bank, which are concerned with areas in which policy coherence is needed.

■ DFID helped to build capacity in developing countries to prepare for and participate in international negotiations on trade, investment and other areas.

---

In *Germany*, a regulation ensures the routine examination of all new legislation, by the Ministry for Economic Co-operation and Development (BMZ), for its coherence with development policy. The ministry also has a seat on the Federal Security Council to facilitate the integration of crisis prevention and conflict settlement with development policies. The *Canadian* International Development Agency is often directly involved in consultations with other government departments about non-aid policies related to debt relief, preferential import tariffs, and other areas. The *New Zealand* government is explicitly committed to ensuring that the policies it formulates are consistent and coherent. *Sweden* has appointed a Parliamentary Commission on enhanced policy coherence for poverty reduction in the era of globalisation. *Norway* is developing a Poverty Action Plan including policy coherence. *Finland* emphasises poverty reduction and collective security in its Comprehensive Policy on Relations with Developing Countries.

The *European Union* deploys considerable staff resources in its complex structures of decision-making. In addition to policy co-ordination within the European Commission (EC), the EU must also co-ordinate the policies of the EC with those of its member governments. Once acceptable common positions are reached, the process of moving forward towards greater coherence is facilitated. An example concerns proposed reforms in the design of food security policy, including food aid, separating it from a supply-led disposal of surplus food stocks. Another is the Everything-but-Arms initiative, eliminating import restrictions towards least developed countries.

**The international community is emphasising that effective poverty reduction calls for involving women in consultations,...**

A basic principle of policy coherence is to broaden decision-making processes so that women, as well as men, especially those who are poor, have full input into the definition of what is important and what needs should have priority. The United Nations World Conference on Women in Beijing in 1995 agreed that "governments and other actors should promote an active and visible policy of mainstreaming a gender perspective in all policies and programmes". Policy analysis should consider the different opportunities available to women and men, their potentials and the effects on them of any development activities. An important benefit from action of this sort is that involving women will positively impact poverty reduction, since women have a key role in poverty reduction, as noted above. Particular attention must be paid to the range of barriers that have kept women out of international negotiations and other formal decision-making positions.

Choosing partner countries selectively and allocating aid where it will be most effective can be an important instrument for policy coherence within OECD governments. Coherence, in this context, refers to the allocation of ODA resources according to criteria primarily related to reducing poverty and not to objectives in other areas such as trade, foreign policy and national security.

*... allocating aid according to poverty criteria...*

The DAC has promoted support for enhancing the institutional capacity of partner countries in international trade negotiations by developing a set of Good Practices. These are designed to enhance the co-ordination of such support, while ensuring that capacity-building is demand-led and locally-owned. Another effort to promote co-ordination is the Integrated Framework for Trade-Related Technical Assistance, a partnership among six multilateral agencies (WTO, World Bank, IMF, UNDP, UNCTAD, ITC) working to co-ordinate support for the integration of trade and related technical assistance and capacity-building into national poverty reduction strategies of least developed countries.

*... and promoting institutional capacity-building for trade...*

There is a further need to establish mechanisms whereby the processes of international negotiations assure full participation by the partner countries in formulating and reaching agreements. Norway, Sweden and Switzerland have provided capacity-building in debt management, budget and comptroller systems. Australia provides technical assistance related to global trade negotiations.

*... and debt management.*

## Policy areas

Coherence across the full range of policies of the OECD countries is important because they impact on so many different dimensions of North-South relations. The number of ways in which coherence could influence poverty reduction is vast, but for practical purposes and taking into account the likelihood of achieving changes, only those most important for these *Guidelines* need to be selected. The proposed priority areas are listed under six thematic headings in Box 16 and then briefly presented in the same order in the remainder of this part.[1]

*The priority areas for policy coherence reforms are listed here, and each area annotated through the remainder of Part 4.*

---

### Box 16. Areas of policy coherence – a short list

■ **International trade and foreign direct investment**
   International trade regime
   Preferential trading arrangements
   Export finance
   Trade in services
   Foreign direct investment
   Transfer of technology (including ICT)

■ **International finance**
   Financial sector reform
   Portfolio investment
   Debt relief

■ **Food and agriculture**
   Food trade and agricultural policies
   Food aid and food security
   Agricultural research

■ **Natural resources and environmental sustainability**
   Global pollution
   Trade and investment
   Use of renewable natural resources:
   – Fisheries
   – Forestry

■ **Social issues**
   Labour standards
   Immigration
   Global public health
   Illegal drugs

■ **Governance and conflict**
   Democracy and human rights
   Corporate governance
   Conflict prevention and resolution
   Arms trade

---

## International trade and foreign direct investment

International trade is a powerful tool for reducing poverty. The potential impact on the national incomes and welfare of developing countries, produced by eliminating or reducing remaining restrictions on imports, would dwarf recent ODA flows. While some trade liberalisation reforms have been undertaken, further reforms are possible and necessary, although they become progressively more politically difficult when key policy objectives like employment and regional development are affected. The major trade and investment policy areas of importance for enhanced policy coherence are *i)* the overall international trade regime, *ii)* preferential trading arrangements, *iii)* trade in services, *iv)* export finance, *v)* foreign direct investment, and *vi)* transfer of technology. Agricultural subsidies and food trade are covered below.

*i.* **The international trade regime** includes several provisions, which particularly limit the access of processed products from developing nations to markets in OECD and other countries. Even though average tariff levels have been reduced to historically low levels, *tariff peaks* remain for products in which developing countries are most competitive. Another issue is *tariff escalation* with increasing rates for more processed goods, which impede industrial exports from developing countries. Further, limiting regulations are seen in *non-tariff barriers* like product standards and regulations, rules-of-origin and product labelling, discriminating subsidies and related countervailing duties, anti-dumping duties and non-transparent government procurement, including aid tying and shipping.

*ii.* Trade policy coherence is complicated by the intrinsic incoherence of various **preferential trading arrangements,** which are mainly to the advantage of middle-income and transition countries. The benefits have been limited by excluding sensitive products in some sectors, in which poor countries have the best opportunity to expand and diversify their exports, and they can be withdrawn unilaterally if imports from any country increase significantly. Moreover, these schemes are often too complex for weak administrations to understand and apply.

*iii.* **Export finance** policies and practices – including guarantees – have an impact on debt, sustainable development and poverty reduction. OECD Ministers have mandated the Export Credit Group (ECG) to strengthen measures to ensure that export credits are consistent with international agreements on sustainable development, and – in the case of HIPCs – are not used for unproductive purposes. Further, the ECG has recommended measures both to deter bribery in the credits themselves and to deny such credits where the relevant export contracts involve bribery.[2]

*iv.* **Trade in services** is expanding much faster than trade in goods, partly because technological advances have made many kinds of services tradable for the first time. The WTO General Agreement on Trade in Services (GATS) is a major step towards establishing a rules-based multilateral system for trade in services. Although it has accomplished little actual liberalisation of trade in services, it did create a framework for future negotiations in separate service sectors. Market access in the OECD countries is a major coherence issue, since their commitments under the GATS are far from complete, especially in the area of labour services where developing countries might have good prospects.

*v.* **Foreign direct investment** (FDI) in developing countries has grown extremely rapidly in recent years. It has mainly benefited a few emerging market economies in East Asia and Latin America.[3] Low-income countries lack the policy and institutional environments, infrastructure, economic dynamism and market size of better-off nations, which are needed to attract FDI. Much of what they do receive is channelled into extractive industries with limited or even negative impacts on political and social stability, and on poverty. Any negotiating process towards an international agreement on investment rules, which could secure enhanced access to development finance, needs to include developing countries as fully-fledged partners.

*vi.* **The transfer of technology** to developing countries usually accompanies FDI, but also takes place in other ways. The relevant WTO agreement TRIPS[4] regulates the transfer of technology. It was concluded to stimulate capital investment in research and development of new technology, but not with a view to reducing poverty. A number of policy coherence issues have arisen to do with patents affecting global public goods like forms of life, bio-diversity and life-saving drugs (see Social issues below). A related issue concerns *information and communication technology* (ICT), which could create major opportunities for developing countries. But there is a risk that the domination of ICT by developed countries may worsen global economic inequalities. Special efforts in education and training and specific action to facilitate access to the technologies, infrastructure, market conditions, legal frameworks and the required knowledge are all necessary.

## International finance

The decade of the 1990s witnessed a major increase in the flows of international capital to developing countries, in which private capital became much more significant in total than ODA. Factors accounting for this phenomenon include deregulation, regional integration, and advanced information technology. Although this has provided much needed capital, mostly for the larger and more developed of the developing countries, it has also led to an increased volatility of flows, to debt crises and to wider financial crises. Coherence issues occur concerning : *i)* financial sector reform, *ii)* portfolio investment and *iii)* debt relief to poor countries. Foreign direct investment and export financing have been considered above.

*i.* **Financial sector reform** is important, both nationally and internationally, for enhancing incentives for efficient investment and economic growth and to minimise the risk of financial crises. Orderly sequencing of reforms is crucial and should include a prudential regulation of the banking sector, institutional capacity-building and better co-ordination between exchange rate policy, monetary policy, and controls or taxes on capital flows. A related issue of concern is that developing countries should adequately be represented in international forums discussing reforms in financial architecture.

*ii.* **Portfolio investment** provides valuable financial capital, mainly to middle-income developing countries with fair to good credit ratings. But short-term capital movements are a major cause of volatility, which, in recent financial crises around the world, has increased poverty. Related problems are capital flight, bank secrecy and tax havens. Policy coherence means recognising these risks and installing adequate regulatory measures integrated into international financial architecture and into the monetary policies of countries that either import or export capital.

*iii.* **Debt relief** for HIPCs is internationally recognised as necessary if poverty is to be reduced. To be effective it has to be additional, considering both the extent to which the debt could and would have been serviced without relief and the risk of reducing other forms of ODA and other financial transfer. The amounts of debt relief must be sufficient for debt sustainability, for investment in economic growth and for adequate social and other expenditures of importance for reducing poverty.

Creditors must consider the risks and responsibilities involved in making loans to poor countries, and must share the consequent costs of failed credits.

## Food and agriculture

The World Food Summit goal of halving the number of the world's undernourished people by 2015 calls for increased food production, in particular by smallholders in net food-importing developing countries. This is of major importance for enhancing food security and the incomes of poor women and men. Issues of coherence arise in several areas in food and agriculture: *i)* food trade and agricultural policies, *ii)* food aid and food security, and *iii)* agricultural research and biotechnology.

*i.* **Food trade and agricultural policies** are of crucial importance because they are politically sensitive and directly affect people who are poor and who lack food security. The effect on world food prices and, thus, on the import costs faced by net food-importing developing countries, of reducing domestic and export subsidies is particularly important. Most of these countries have become more dependent on food imports and are increasingly vulnerable to rising prices and, indirectly, are likely to be affected by agricultural policies in OECD countries. While higher food prices would in the long run tend to stimulate their own food production and make them less dependent on food imports. Food prices may fall as a result of increased production and exports by low-cost producers, but, in the short term, poor countries with food deficits could face severe problems in food security.

*ii.* **Food security and food aid** have become substantially more coherent areas of development co-operation; there has been a shift from simply disposing of surplus food stocks towards more flexible forms of food aid. These include the greater availability of grant money for purchases in local or regional markets and more attention to avoiding disruption in them, a more appropriate product mix and better forecasting of needs. Some problems persist, such as using food aid to support domestic farm prices, or the lack of adequate supplies of both food and cash for food security, and incoherent policies among major food exporters.

*iii.* **Agricultural research** is crucial for agricultural development and food security. *Biotechnology* has a particularly large potential for poverty reduction if applied in developing countries. But transferring this technology to poor countries presents a major challenge calling for greater policy coherence. This is for two main reasons:

■ Private sector research is driven by market demand in rich countries, rather than by the needs of poor people and countries for whom special measures ensuring food security and safety are needed.

■ There is considerable concern about food safety and the long-term environmental, health and socio-economic impact of using gene technology. This raises issues of labelling, traceability and international regulatory mechanisms to ensure that new technologies are properly tested for possible adverse effects.[6] International standards and arrangements for mutual recognition could help avoid the emergence of new trade barriers in this area. Support for building effective legal, administrative and scientific capacities is important in order to enable developing countries to take advantage of the opportunities and to control the risks of gene technology.

## Natural resources and environmental sustainability

Many of the policy issues involving the management of natural resources and the environment must primarily be dealt with by the partner countries. However, some issues are regional or global in scope and involve matters of policy coherence. Among these are: *i)* global pollution, *ii)* trade and investment impact, and *iii)* use of renewable natural resources.

*i.* **Global pollution** perpetuates climate change and a reduction of the ozone layer.[6] As a result, poor people in developing countries will experience greater hardship and vulnerability. Emissions have so far been greatest in the OECD area, but fast-growing developing countries are catching up. The rapid rate at which climate change is taking place is of particular concern, since the ability of societies and ecosystems to adapt is limited. Global environmental pollution raises important coherence issues for OECD governments, both in relation to any unilateral actions they may take to reduce global warming and to restore the ozone layer, and in relation to the positions they take at relevant international forums.

*ii.* **Trade and investment** are normally not causes of poverty or of environmental degradation, but can exacerbate, or bring into the open, existing distortions or inequities in resource endowments. Trade rules and policies, market access and product characteristics affect the complex links between natural resource management and poverty reduction. Trade and investment raise the value of natural resources, reinforcing incentives for efficient and sustainable management. But when property rights are unclearly defined and regulations governing the extraction of natural resources are weak or poorly enforced, the increased demand for natural resources, resulting from openness to trade, can accelerate the unsustainable use of resources. When access to natural resources is highly inequitable, the benefits from trade can aggravate income inequalities and further marginalise poor people.

Foreign direct investment often includes the transfer of modern technologies and methods of production; these, in turn, lead to improved efficiency in the use of resources and reduced pollution and waste. However, it can sometimes involve the transfer of polluting production and extraction processes (manufacturing, mining and oil) to developing countries with negative environmental, health and other social effects, especially for poor people.[7] A related issue is the export of hazardous waste, which must be strictly monitored to be coherent with sustainable development.[8]

*iii.*The accelerated **use of renewable natural resources** in developing countries may be unsustainable and involve economic interests of OECD countries. Fisheries and forestry are two major examples:

■ *Fish* are often important sources of revenue, livelihoods and nutrition in developing coastal countries, especially for communities in small island states. Although they often target different stocks, foreign factory fleet fishing may reduce local catches. In some cases, foreign fleets are subsidised and may not pay the full costs for the fish they catch and fishing grounds run the risk of becoming overexploited. Existing or potential fish-processing industries, which are apt to involve women, may be adversely affected, and a significant potential for poverty reduction lost. In Asia and Latin America, a related issue is the large-scale conversion of mangroves to unsustainable shrimp farming ponds. Policy coherence calls for special assessments and measures to ensure that bilateral agreements on large-scale fishing in the waters of developing countries, and on shrimp farming, contribute to sustainable poverty reduction. Access fees and export revenues should be used to improve fishery and coastal management and for pro-poor development in coastal communities.

■ *Forest* depletion can be perpetuated by the exploitation of natural resource forests for timber, especially in the absence of effective trade and logging regulation. In the poorest countries or regions, another major cause of forest depletion is the stripping of woodlands for fuel-wood by poor people with no access to alternative sources of energy. Many species of wildlife are endangered by logging, hunting and capture for export.

### Social issues

If poverty is to be reduced, then social policies must also be coherent, both internationally and nationally. The most important issues arise in: *i)* labour standards, *ii)* immigration, *iii)* global public health, and *iv)* illegal drugs.

*i.* Internationally recognised, core **labour standards** are included in the revised OECD *Guidelines for Multinational Enterprises*, which apply to OECD-based investors, and to their worldwide affiliates, including those in developing countries. The ILO has adopted a "decent work agenda" in co-operation with WTO, UNCTAD, the World Bank, the IMF and the OECD, which links rights at work and social dialogue with employment policies and social protection. Eliminating the worst forms of child labour calls for development co-operation in support of policies to ensure that children have full access to education and that parents can afford to spare their work and incomes.[9]

*ii.* Member countries of the OECD, while encouraging poor countries to establish open markets, have, at the same time, established restrictive **immigration** policies, which close their borders to all except skilled professional labour. Because developing countries frequently lack adequate opportunities for such people, these selective immigration policies contribute to the depletion of human resources. "Brain drain" is an important coherence issue. Development co-operation policies in support of increasing employment opportunities in partner countries may contribute to resolving the problem.

*iii.* In global **public health,** coherence has to do with research and pricing of medicines. Biomedical research takes place mainly in OECD countries and is primarily directed by markets, i.e. towards diseases in these countries. Some of these are also serious health problems in developing countries. However, less than 10% of global public and private sector health research funds are devoted to diseases or conditions accounting for 90% of the global disease burden.[10] These afflict mainly poor people and poor countries and they cannot afford the available medicines that can save or prolong lives, for example against HIV/AIDS. This has led to a debate about intellectual property rights where they conflict with important social issues. Although the TRIPS agreement under the WTO calls for general protection of these rights, it also provides for exceptions for the protection of public health. Some important steps to address these problems – including research incentives and affordability – are being taken, but major issues remain to be resolved concerning the further development of appropriate international frameworks.

According to WHO estimates, smoking causes around 4 million deaths every year throughout the world. This death toll is projected to increase to 10 million by 2030, 70% of which will be in developing countries. This is a terrible human cost as well as an economic shock to poor countries because of the loss of productive people and the burden on public health systems. OECD governments may consider promoting policy measures to discourage smoking and increase awareness of its health risks in developing countries, as they do domestically, and to enhance social responsibilities on the part of tobacco companies.

*iv.* **Illegal drugs** are closely related to poverty. Farmers often grow the plants used to produce illicit drugs because they have few good alternatives. Policies that aim only to interdict and eliminate the trade may have negative consequences for the livelihoods of poor rural communities. They will only be effective in the long run if the growers can find other sustainable sources of livelihood. Illegal drugs (and minerals such as diamonds) have become major sources of revenue for criminal organisations, warlords and armies waging internal wars. Profits from this illicit industry are increasingly being used to finance armed conflicts. Thus, there is a strong link between the struggle to reduce the drug trade and efforts to promote the prevention and resolution of armed conflict.

## Governance and conflict

It is now generally agreed that sustainable poverty reduction requires good governance, economic and political stability and peace. The main coherence issues in this policy area concern *i)* democracy and human rights, *ii)* corporate governance, *iii)* conflict prevention and resolution, and *iv)* arms trade.

*i.* Empowerment of the poor through participatory **democracy and human rights** is central to reducing poverty. When OECD governments prioritise the reduction of poverty and support participatory democracy and respect for human rights, policies are generally coherent. On the other hand, when deficient governance, a lack of transparency and corruption in partner countries are addressed, difficulties with political sensitivities and with commercial or other foreign policy considerations can lead to a certain lack of coherence.

*ii.* Policy-makers are increasingly recognising the importance of **corporate governance** issues and the evil effects of corruption. Nevertheless, much room remains for greater co-operation in the design of coherent policies among the OECD area policy communities that deal with grand corruption in international business, petty corruption as it affects the poor, competition policy, harmful tax competition and money laundering.[11]

*iii.* Poverty reduction is closely associated with **conflict prevention and resolution.** The lack of opportunity or skills to secure employment, the inability to pay school fees, the scarcity of food and water, and the lack of access to health care may be substantial inducements to poor men and boys to join armed groups. Policy coherence issues can arise if the causes of conflicts breaking out or persisting are connected to commercial, foreign policy or national security interests of OECD countries. Doing the utmost to prevent and to resolve conflicts, including support for the United Nations and its peacekeeping forces, is a major plank in the platform of coherent policies for poverty reduction.

*iv.* The 1990s have witnessed a marked increase in the international **arms trade** – particularly in small arms, light weapons and land mines – which has massively increased the number of poor and disabled women, men and children. The annual figure for the arms trade is estimated at about $10 billion, most of it coming from a dozen or so countries. Abating this trade is a major challenge for OECD policy coherence.

# Notes

1. An extended, but still incomplete and only illustrative, list of areas for policy coherence is included in the annexed checklist, which is designed as a compact standalone document. Because it addresses a wider audience than these *Guidelines*, it is structured in a different way and includes development co-operation issues covered in other parts of these *Guidelines*.

2. See ECG Action Statement (December 2000) with reference to the OECD Convention on Combating Bribery of Foreign Public Officials in International Business Transactions.

3. Twenty-three such countries account for 90% of FDI. Of these, China and Brazil alone accounted for one-half of FDI flows to developing countries in 1998, and ten middle-income countries for 70%.

4. Trade-related intellectual property rights.

5. *The Cartagena Protocol on Biosafety* to the *Convention on Biological Diversity*, adopted in Montreal, Canada in 2000, is to enter into force upon ratification.

6. In 1996, the Intergovernmental Panel on Climate Change (IPCC) concluded that "the balance of evidence suggests a discernible human influence on global climate". Later research has strengthened this conclusion. See IPCC Third Assessment Report *Climate Change 2001: The Scientific Basis*, Shanghai 2001 (*www.meto.gov.uk/sec5/CR_div/ipcc/wg1/WGI-SPM.pdf*)

7. *Foreign Direct Investment and the Environment*, OECD, Paris, 1999.

8. This is regulated by the Basel Convention on the Control of Transboundary Movements of Hazardous Wastes and their Disposal (1989). Similar problems have occurred with aid-supplied pesticides causing hazards to users and environmental contamination. See Guidelines for Aid Agencies on Pest and Pesticide Management, OECD/DAC *Guidelines on Aid and Environment* No. 6. 1995.

9. See *Declaration and Decisions on International Investment and Multinational Enterprises: Basic Texts*. OECD, Paris, November 2000; *International Trade and Core Labour Standards*, OECD, Paris, 2000; *ILO Declaration of Fundamental Principles and Rights at Work* (1998), *ILO Convention on the Worst Forms of Child Labour* (1999).

10. *The 10/90 Report on Health Research 2000*, Global Forum for Health Research, WHO, *www.globalforumhealth.org*

11. The OECD hosts and provides services for the Financial Action Task Force (FATF), an independent body which has made major strides in international co-operation to counter money-laundering operations.

# Annex

# An illustrative checklist on policy coherence for poverty reduction

*"Improved policy coherence within OECD countries is also necessary if developing countries are to take full advantage of the opportunities of globalisation: OECD will develop a Checklist on Policy Coherence to assist its Member countries in this area. The OECD will also deepen its analytical work on the linkages between trade liberalisation, economic growth and poverty reduction."* "Shaping Globalisation", Communiqué of the meeting of the OECD Council at Ministerial level, OECD, Paris, 27 June 2000.

## Why focus coherence efforts on poverty reduction?

The concept of coherence across the spectrum of policy areas has gathered increasing support in high-level OECD discussions over the years. Governments have multiple and often competing priorities. Poverty reduction will not always outweigh other priorities in the decision-making of OECD Members, but there is now a more evident readiness to give it a high ranking. Widespread political acceptance and support of the poverty reduction objective has been expressed recently at very high levels – at the OECD, among the G-8 Heads of State and at the World Bank, the IMF and the United Nations.

Why should poverty reduction, rather than some other broad policy objective, merit the central place in coherence efforts? No less than 1.2 billion people – a fifth of the world's population and one-quarter of all people in developing countries – live in extreme poverty, on less than $1 per day. Nearly three billion people – half the world's population – live on less than $2 a day. OECD political leaders – including the G-8 Heads of State and OECD Ministers – have recognised poverty as a Global Public "Bad", not only on economic and humanitarian grounds but also as a source of dysfunction and disorder in developing societies and in the world generally. The resulting political instability, environmental degradation, disruptive migrations and similar phenomena pose threats to the interests of OECD Member countries. This recognition has spread. International Development Goals,[1] including that of reducing the incidence of extreme poverty by half by 2015, have been adopted as a common frame of reference by the IMF, the World Bank and the UN, as well as the G-8 leaders.

Critics of globalisation, both within and outside the OECD area, see poverty in the midst of plenty as the most prominent manifestation of globalisation's uneven effects. Many of its proponents, too, well aware that rapid economic change on a global scale can produce both "winners" and "losers", perceive how it can marginalise both the poorest countries and substantial proportions of populations in middle-income developing countries, when asymmetrical economic growth generates income inequality. Such effects need not occur, but if they do, they imperil globalisation and its manifold benefits.

Policy coherence is needed, therefore, to ensure that globalisation works for all. Coherent policies can overcome the asymmetries that creep into the globalisation process, often because of policy *in*coherence in both developed and developing countries. With its profound benefits of growth and economic integration, globalisation is a friend, not an enemy of poverty reduction. In adopting policy coherence for poverty reduction as a key objective, developed countries will generate broader confidence and support for globalisation as a process that increases welfare in the world at large.

---

1. See the list of Millennium Development Goals, page 17.

## Box 17. The dimensions of policy coherence

The coherence challenge has a number of dimensions that need to be addressed in a synchronised manner, while recognising that full coherence is never a realistic outcome.

- *Policy co-ordination* means getting the various institutional and managerial systems, which formulate policy, to work together.

- *Policy consistency* means ensuring that individual policies are not internally contradictory, and avoiding policies that conflict with reaching for a given policy objective, in this case international poverty reduction.

- *Policy coherence* goes further; it involves the systematic promotion of mutually reinforcing policy actions across government departments and agencies creating synergies towards achieving the defined objective.

## Why a checklist?

A wide range of policies of developed countries bears directly on poverty in developing countries. If coherent, they can help to alleviate it. It is axiomatic that coherent policies are more effective than incoherent ones, but the challenge is not a small one. The specific issues most often involve domestic interest groups and government agencies with primary goals other than poverty reduction. Conflict may occur between efforts to meet the demands of domestic interests and commitments to reduce poverty in developing countries. Furthermore, development agencies often hold weak positions compared with other government entities and public or private interests associated with issues – like trade, investment, agriculture and national security – on which coherence efforts could be most effective.

Most governments have not systematically promoted coherence in policy formulation across ministerial or departmental lines. Officials and institutions, unless driven by inescapable instructions from centres of government and held accountable for coherent results, have tended to guard their territories reflexively. However, in recent years, this has begun to change. In a widening range of fields, policy-makers in developed countries recognise that they cannot adequately advise their governments on core policy issues, or engage in international discussions and negotiations, without taking into account the impact on and reactions of developing countries, including the poorest. An articulate NGO movement which reminds governments and the public of the impacts of policies on poor countries is also an important factor here. Against this background, there is now a more widely shared concern across different policy communities to address the impact of policies on poverty reduction.

Assessing the coherence of policies requires criteria and knowledge about the mechanisms that link a particular policy to international poverty. It needs careful analysis of each policy's role, its impact on poverty and where within governments it can be changed to enhance coherence. Such analysis requires adequate resources in both aid agencies and other policy communities. The results should form part of the brief to policy-makers engaged in inter-ministerial deliberations and international negotiations.

The ensuing policy adjustments for greater coherence – some but not all of which may be fairly easy to accomplish once an effort is made and incoherence comes into focus – will likely emerge from a political process. Easy or not, however, the key task is to make the case for them. That demands solid analysis, serious efforts to transmit the necessary knowledge to policy-makers and stakeholders, and attention to providing reliable, sound information to the media and civil society, which will play a major role in informing and educating the public.

## Making policy coherence work

Achieving policy coherence requires:

- Clear political direction from national leaders and strong management from the centre of government.
- Clear official statements of goals.

■ Effective consultation and strong links between public agencies, private interests and civil society, including NGOs. Development agencies probably have better links to many key NGOs (including those in developing countries) than other parts of government. Hence, they have this resource to offer to finance ministries, trade ministries and the like.

■ Development of institutional capacity within governments, both to analyse what coherence means in specific, practical policy areas and to pursue it in effective co-operative mechanisms within governments.

■ Making aid agencies equal partners in those institutional arrangements.

■ More attention by aid agencies to links with multilateral organisations, along with the acquiescence of the government agencies and departments that normally deal with those institutions.

## An illustrative checklist – a tool for governments in seeking to promote policy coherence for poverty reduction

This checklist is designed to encourage and assist the governments of OECD Member countries to establish the capacities and systems that can ensure policy coherence for poverty reduction in their decision-making processes. It contains suggestions and guidelines only, because the individual governments of OECD Member countries will tend to design and pursue policy coherence systems in very different ways.

The checklist has two parts. The first, procedural part suggests steps for instituting a coherence system. Flexibility is important here. Policy environments and priorities can change rapidly, and an effective system should be able to respond to these changes without constant revision of the system itself. The second part of the checklist covers a series of illustrative strategic substantive items for systematic policy review. They will require almost constant revision and updating. Policy issues are often time-bound. Tomorrow's coherence issues will not necessarily look the same as today's, even if poverty reduction remains the constant focus. Moreover, this part of the checklist is incomplete, limited arbitrarily to a single illustrative page. Individual governments can and will produce more comprehensive – and often different – checklist items.

## Measures to be considered for enhancing policy coherence for poverty reduction: an illustrative checklist

### A. Organisational and procedural measures

■ Formally committing to the Millennium Development Goals with:

– A clear official statement on the poverty reduction goal and its priority.
– Public information programmes explaining the importance of international poverty reduction.

■ Providing government agencies with analytical capacity to evaluate poverty reduction linkages in their policy areas and to identify priority issues, and:

– Linking these capacities and priorities to the Millennium Development Goals.
– Ensuring inclusion of gender analysis in all relevant policy studies.

■ Establishing inter-ministerial/inter-agency processes, to screen policies and decisions *vis-à-vis* poverty reduction goals, with a lead agency and/or "core" group capable of getting results. Such processes might include:

– Information exchange procedures between policy communities.
– Reporting systems, so that coherence failures within government and in the field become known to policy-makers and are used to make corrections.
– Training and awareness-building throughout the government on poverty reduction and the adaptation of various policies to contribute to it.
– Appropriate, regular contacts with and input from private sector and civil society.

### B. An illustrative list of substantive issues for policy review

■ Objectives for international negotiations, with the aim of enhancing policy coherence for poverty reduction, including on trade, agriculture, finance, environment, migration, labour standards, governance, conflict and related policy areas.

■ Full participation by poor countries in all international negotiations of relevance for poverty reduction.

■ Trade policy measures (*e.g.* anti-dumping, countervailing duty and safeguard actions, preferential trading arrangements, export finance and disciplines) and their coherence with poverty reduction goals.

■ Tariff schedules and their coherence with poverty reduction goals (*e.g.* tariff escalation and tariff peaks that discourage imports from poor countries).

■ Domestic subsidy policies for possible coherence implications in their international effects (*e.g.* in energy, agriculture and fisheries).

■ Rules of origin in customs law and procedure, with a focus on adapting them to the globalisation of production.

■ Domestic standards regulation, with a focus on access for imports from poor countries and regions, consistent with principles of product safety and public health, with use of the precautionary approach based on scientific risk assessment and insulated from protectionist pressures.

■ International financial policies, with a view to promoting pro-poor growth and investments and minimising the risks of financial volatility and crises with severe poverty impact.

■ Debt relief arrangements, to ensure debt sustainability of poor countries, leaving adequate fiscal resources for poverty-reducing expenditures and involving creditors in appropriate risk-sharing.

■ Capacity-building efforts in developing countries, to ensure adequate focus on the poorest countries and to enhance co-ordination with programmes of other countries and international organisations. Give special attention to coherence and efficiency among programmes of different national agencies and ministries.

■ Financial, technical and policy input to promote the use of *information and communication technology* (ICT) in poor countries.

■ National health research and aid budgets, to increase research on diseases endemic in poor countries, in co-operation with other countries and the private sector, in ways which provide incentives and funding for international programmes to make effective pharmaceuticals available to poor people.

■ TRIPS-related issues of policy coherence (*e.g.* patents affecting global public goods like forms of life, bio-diversity and life-saving medicines, indigenous knowledge and innovations, geographical attributions).

■ Food aid and hunger policies, with a view towards better international co-ordination of programmes, considering specifically the poverty reduction aspects of adjustments to liberalised farm trade.

■ Poverty reduction and conflict prevention elements in policies relating to international arms trade, with appropriate guidelines.

■ Policies on conflict and security issues in poor countries in order to enhance co-ordination and reduce inconsistency in developed country responses.

■ Support for capacity-building in effective, democratic and transparent governance and for combating corruption in low-income countries.

■ Consistency and adequacy of corporate governance policies (*e.g.* concerning corruption in international business, the drug trade, tax havens, money-laundering, regulation of competition).

## Box 18. Areas of policy coherence — an extended list

**1. International trade in goods and services; foreign direct investment (FDI); related policies**

International negotiation issues

  Tariffs

  Non-tariff trade barriers (NTBs)

    Standards for products and services

    Regulation of goods and services trade

    Government procurement; tied aid

    Rules of origin

  Subsidies and countervailing duties

  Preferential trading arrangements

  Anti-dumping regimes

  Intellectual property rights (IPRs)

  International investment agreements

  Official export credits and credit guarantees (incl. mixed credits and agricultural credits)

  Capacity-building

  Corporate governance

  Competition policy

  Maximising benefits of FDI in poor countries

  Tax havens and harmful tax competition

  Technology transfer issues

    Production and trade of generic drugs and their availability to the poor (partly IPR-related)

    ICT: "Digital Divide" issues

**2. Food and agriculture**

Agricultural policies

Agricultural trade

Food security

Food aid

Hunger

Agricultural research, including biotechnology

Genetically modified organisms (GMOs) and trade in their products

**3. Natural resources and environmental sustainability**

Global environment (*e.g.* climate change, ozone layer, biodiversity)

Regional, subregional environment (*e.g.* acid deposition, marine pollution)

Local environment as both a sustainability and a public health issue (*e.g.* air, water, soil pollution)

Sustainable exploitation of renewable resources (*e.g.* fisheries, forests)

Use of non-renewable resources and minimising adverse environmental and social impacts

The impacts of trade and investment on the environment

**4. Governance issues**

Democracy and human rights

Transparency

Responsive public institutions

The fight against corruption

Civil service organisation and professionalism

Labour rights

**5. Conflict and security issues**

Conflict prevention and resolution

Arms trade

**6. Social issues**

Education and training

Social safety nets

Public health systems.

Migration

Public health issues like tropical diseases, tobacco

**7. Broad economic and financial issues**

Macroeconomic policy

Structural surveillance policies

The international financial architecture

Money-laundering

# 5 Institutional change and development for mainstreaming poverty reduction, partnership and policy coherence

## Introduction

Tackling poverty effectively calls for mainstreaming poverty reduction throughout agency policies and operations, for working as good partners, and for improving policy coherence across DAC Member governments.[1] These are key challenges for development co-operation agencies. Successfully addressing them calls for important changes in their institutions: their organisational structures, incentives, practices, systems and cultures. Retooling agency institutional capacity and aligning their management systems behind these challenges will enhance efforts to implement these *Guidelines* – and deliver on development goals.

Part 5 focuses on the organisational setting of development agencies and presents options for strengthening institutional alignment behind poverty reduction, partnership and policy coherence objectives.[2] Institutional change in public administrative systems is complex, often calling for creativity, innovation and strong leadership. The DAC and its Members will continue to explore ways to promote institutional change as experience deepens and additional good practice comes to light.

**Mainstreaming poverty reduction, partnership and policy coherence calls for important changes within agencies themselves: their organisational systems, structures, incentives and cultures.**

## Why look inside our own institutions?

In 1998 the DAC Network on Poverty Reduction (POVNET) commissioned a review assessing the performance of each bilateral agency in addressing poverty reduction. The findings of the *DAC Scoping Study of Donor Poverty Reduction Policies and Practices* (OECD, Paris, 1999) revealed that agencies' performance – in terms of poverty reduction commitment, focus and follow-through – fell short of their stated aims.

The study highlighted three problems experienced in varying degrees:

- A lack of clear leadership commitment to poverty reduction, resulting in multiple, competing agency objectives, and a lack of focus in management systems and controls and in country programming.

- Institutional rules, management practices and incentive systems that tended to consolidate agency control functions, perpetuated disbursement pressures, inhibited interaction with other development partners, discouraged more integrated, cross-cutting approaches and maintained supply-led approaches to programming.

- Evaluation and performance management systems focused on inputs and measurable outputs, with few links to agency or staff accountability for achieving agency or development goals.

**Past agency poverty reduction performance has fallen short, often because the agency has not been fully aligned – in an organisational sense – behind the poverty reduction goal.**

These problems are indicative of institutions whose structures, systems and cultures are not yet fully aligned behind the goals they have set out to achieve. In order to implement the poverty reduction agenda agreed by DAC Members and spelled out in these *Guidelines*, substantial changes – which will vary depending on agency contexts – will be needed.[3] Development agencies do have other objectives as well, but to the extent that poverty is a key or central objective, such changes will assume greater importance.

## Getting definitions and concepts right

A development agency is, in the first instance, an organisation. In order to understand how agencies might change from within, it is important to understand what an organisation is, how it works, and how it can work most effectively.

***What is meant by "organisations"?*** Organisations are complex social systems made up of four closely inter-related components:

- The people – leadership, management and staff.

- The work – activities performed by employees.

- The formal organisation – structures, processes and systems that organise activities and guide people in the performance of their work.

- The informal organisation (or organisational culture) – organisational values, attitudes and beliefs, unofficial channels of communication and lines of influence, and accepted standards of behaviour.

Organisations also have a vision and a strategy that enable them to move in a particular direction and to achieve specific objectives.

**Development agencies that achieve their institutional goals are those in which all the components of the organisation – its strategy, work, staff, culture, and formal and informal systems – are consistent and well-meshed with one another.**

A successful organisation is one that works smoothly in the sense of "organisational fit" or "congruence" or "alignment", which means that all the internal components of the organisation – the strategy, the work, the formal and informal organisational arrangements and the people – are consistent and well-meshed with one another. There is no *one* best structure, or best culture, or best strategy: *what matters is how these components work together*. All too often, organisations imitate other organisations (especially those with which they share common networks or similar pursuits), adopting practices that may not be aligned with their strategy, or that are inconsistent with their existing organisational arrangements. This creates organisational dysfunction, frustrating efforts to achieve goals and objectives.

By way of illustration, in an agency that is fully aligned behind the poverty reduction objective:

- Leadership is committed to poverty reduction and signals this consistently and visibly through words and deeds to staff, partner countries, and the public at large.

- Organisational structure facilitates the degree of staff interaction, co-mingling of expertise and communication flows necessary to deal with poverty in all its dimensions.

- Human resource management (HRM) systems[4] create a supportive organisational and management structure, including appropriate internal incentive systems, to deliver the knowledge, capacity and motivation required for mainstreaming poverty.

- Internal systems and practices – such as staff regulations, personnel manuals, contracting documents, approval and screening procedures – make concrete links and strengthen accountability to the agency's organisational objective of reducing poverty.

- Staff are committed to integrate poverty reduction in their work and to promote it as an important government policy goal when interacting with other parts of government in capitals, in the field or in international fora.

- The poverty reduction objective is integrated throughout the aid system, including in the policies and activities of implementing agencies and consultants, through participation in the governing boards of multilateral development institutions, and in development assistance provided by other parts of government.

**What is meant by "organisational change"?** Organisations change in order to heighten their prospects for success. Successful organisational change depends on:

- Developing a clear, shared vision of the desired end state/future in order to create a commitment to the change.

- Strong leadership that takes charge of the change process.

- Broad-based involvement and participation.

- Widespread communication (permeating all levels), including sharing information about results.

- Aligning the institution's systems and procedures.

- The use of teams.

- Recognising the importance of culture in facilitating or inhibiting change.

A number of development agencies are undergoing institutional change,[5] often to enable them to respond more effectively to the emerging poverty reduction agenda. For example, UNDP, UK/DFID, Sweden/SIDA and the World Bank are implementing change in both their formal and informal organisations, as well as their work. Canada/CIDA, Denmark/Danida, Germany/BMZ and USAID are changing their monitoring and performance management systems. These changes are geared to finding the right "fit" between these agencies' enhanced commitment to poverty reduction, partnership and policy coherence – and their formal structures, systems and processes. Figure 3 illustrates how an agency might begin to fit the various "pieces" of its organisation to the strategic objectives of reducing poverty and working as partners.

> **A number of DAC Members are undergoing institutional change, often to enable them to respond more effectively to the emerging poverty reduction agenda.**

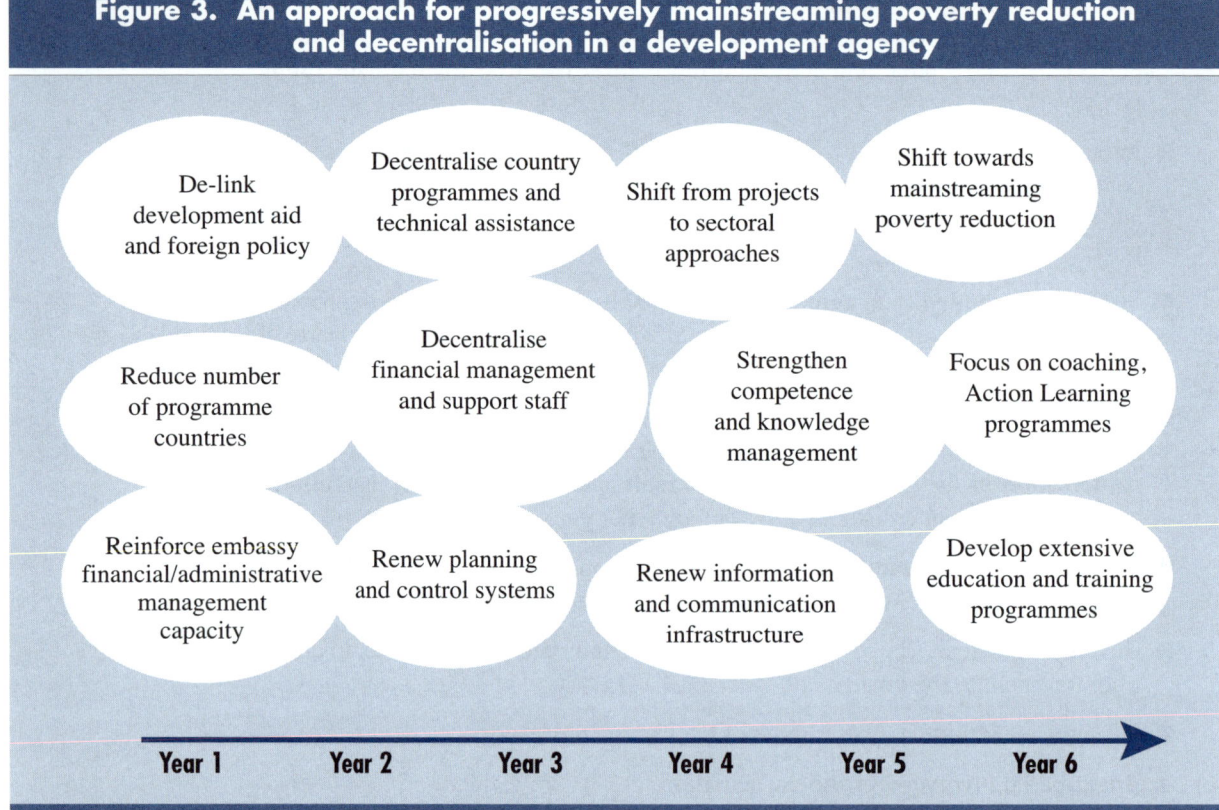

**Figure 3. An approach for progressively mainstreaming poverty reduction and decentralisation in a development agency**

De-link development aid and foreign policy

Decentralise country programmes and technical assistance

Shift from projects to sectoral approaches

Shift towards mainstreaming poverty reduction

Reduce number of programme countries

Decentralise financial management and support staff

Strengthen competence and knowledge management

Focus on coaching, Action Learning programmes

Reinforce embassy financial/administrative management capacity

Renew planning and control systems

Renew information and communication infrastructure

Develop extensive education and training programmes

Year 1    Year 2    Year 3    Year 4    Year 5    Year 6

**Institutional change requires not only adopting new outlooks, reflexes, functions and attitudes, but also "unlearning" existing patterns of behaviour.**

There is no single "blueprint" for fostering institutional change – the process is iterative, and it takes time. It requires not only adopting new outlooks, functions and attitudes – but also "unlearning" existing patterns of behaviour. Each agency will need to carry out its own organisational diagnosis in order to assess how, to what extent, and how quickly it can – and will – make necessary changes in order to implement and achieve their poverty reduction and partnership goals.

The change process will also be affected by the national administrative and domestic political context each agency operates within. Development co-operation agencies are an integral part of complex public administration systems that have rules and procedures that may limit agency options for institutional change. At the same time, agencies are subject to a myriad of influences specific to each DAC Member country, including parliaments and legislatures, politicians, other parts of government, implementing agencies, civil society, NGOs, the business sector, consultants and academic communities. The scope for institutional change will vary across agencies according to the degree of freedom afforded by the public administrative system, domestic political dynamics and the influence of society at large. Mainstreaming a poverty reduction orientation is a challenging process that requires vision, time, proper sequencing, and the capacity to deal with trade-offs in complex institutional settings. Nevertheless, there is considerable scope for aligning agency cultures, structures and practices with the poverty reduction agenda.

# Making sense of diverse institutional set-ups

**Bilateral agencies have different structural and functional paradigms.** DAC member agencies can be categorised into five generic organisational models:

- Agencies located within the Ministry of Foreign Affairs, where development co-operation is grouped together with foreign policy and trade relations in integrated country or regional desks.

- Development co-operation directorates or divisions located within the Ministry of Foreign Affairs.

- Agencies with a lead policy ministry and separate implementing agency(ies).

- Countries where development co-operation is shared among a range of ministries, each of which takes responsibility for a particular aspect of the programme and works with different implementing agencies.

- Autonomous agencies.

Each agency differs markedly in size, scope of operations, range of activities, the staff skill mix and age profile, and the extent to which they are decentralised and/or focused on the poverty reduction goal. They have different ways of working, different organisational cultures, different degrees of autonomy, different comparative advantages and different functional set-ups.

Nevertheless, there are many common features, especially among agencies that share similar structural paradigms or cultural affinities. Figure 4 depicts how the different development agencies compare with one another on a structural basis and, by clustering similar agencies together, suggests where scope for closer collaboration at lower transactions costs may exist. Collaboration among agencies may also be easier where they share common languages, close cultural ties, similar approaches to management and financial control, comparable degrees of decentralisation, and/or close professional ties among their top leadership.

Partnership means going beyond organisational change in individual agencies. It involves change and exchange between and among agencies, and greater collaboration – especially in the field. Learning more about how different agencies work will enable DAC Members to understand how they can work together, and how to work *better* together by exploiting synergies and complementarities.

**Each DAC Member agency is unique: they have different ways of working, different functional set-ups, different organisational cultures, and different goals and objectives.**

**Nevertheless, there are many common features among agencies. Learning more about these similarities, and in general how agencies "work", will enable DAC Members to understand how they can work together, and how to work *better* together.**

## Figure 4. The five generic organisational models of DAC Member development co-operation agencies

### 1. Integrated Ministry of Foreign Affairs

**Ministry of Foreign Affairs**

*North Dept.*
Foreign Policy
Trade
Development
Co-operation

*South Dept.*
Foreign Policy
Trade
Development
Co-operation

**Denmark   Finland   Netherlands**

### 2. Development Co-operation Directorate or Division within the Ministry of Foreign Affairs

**Ministry of Foreign Affairs**

Trade Directorate

Foreign Policy Directorate

Development Co-operation Directorate

**Ireland   Italy   New Zealand   Switzerland**

### 3. Lead Policy Ministry with Separate Implementing Agency(ies)

**Ministry of Foreign Affairs or Autonomous Aid Ministry**

**Implementing Agency(ies)**

**Belgium   Germany   Luxembourg Norway   Sweden**

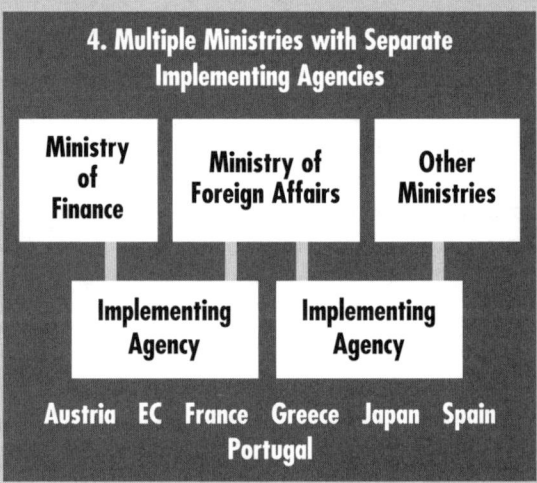

### 4. Multiple Ministries with Separate Implementing Agencies

**Ministry of Finance**

**Ministry of Foreign Affairs**

**Other Ministries**

**Implementing Agency**

**Implementing Agency**

**Austria   EC   France   Greece   Japan   Spain Portugal**

### 5. Autonomous Aid Agency or Ministry

**Ministry/Agency for Development Co-operation**

**Australia   Canada   UK   USA**

*Similar structural set-ups can facilitate closer agency co-ordination and collaboration in the field (research, implementation) or at headquarters (training, information networks). Collaboration may also be easier where agencies share common languages, close cultural ties, similar approaches to management and financial control, and/or comparable degrees of decentralisation.*

# The way ahead: mainstreaming the poverty reduction agenda throughout the agency

Promoting poverty reduction in the policies and activities of an agency will call for much more than just adding a specialised poverty-focused unit. It will require *mainstreaming* a poverty reduction approach throughout the agency, meaning that poverty reduction objectives are taken into account in *all* activities and at *all* organisational levels.

There is no single "right way" to mainstream poverty reduction: what works in one agency may not work in another. Key elements of the organisational set-up that come into play include agency leadership, systems and practices, skills, structures and HRM policies regarding performance management, incentives and training. These are described below, including tips and possible options for implementing change. In considering possible mainstreaming options, it is essential to keep in mind the importance of organisational "fit" – *ensuring that the different pieces of the organisational puzzle are consistent with one another* (for example, that agency performance management and incentives are aligned with the agency's poverty reduction objective).

*"Mainstreaming" poverty reduction throughout an agency means integrating poverty reduction objectives in all activities and at all organisational levels.*

## The role of agency leadership: vision, commitment and creating a culture of change

The commitment of agency leaders and senior management to poverty reduction is pivotal in creating a culture of commitment within the agency. Leadership's role in defining the institution's objectives, values, and sense of mission sets the stage for action. Modelling behaviour at the top is very important: staff look to their leaders for direction, inspiration and guidance. Clear messages from leaders, widely diffused throughout the organisation (by means of statements, speeches and memoranda), and consistent behaviour by senior officials can play an important role in creating a climate of commitment to implementing the poverty reduction agenda – and making rhetoric a reality.

Agency leaders are the prime catalysts for creating a culture of change within their organisations. Change is not easily activated in institutional settings. Agency staff are busy coping with problems, pressures and people: they have little time or interest in changing things. And change is not viewed in a positive light; it is dislocating, unsettling and threatening. In the past, an authoritarian approach to implementing organisational change was common – but it was not always most effective. Change imposed from the top with little staff involvement generates hostility, suspicion and defensiveness and mobilises both overt and covert opposition. It results in changes to the organisation without a change in people's attitudes: *surface change without commitment*.

*Agency leadership plays a key role in creating a culture of commitment within the agency to poverty reduction, and in fostering and managing institutional change.*

Staff must see the need for the change, want the change, and be involved in planning the steps and methods required to effect the change. Organisations that have succeeded in carrying out real behavioural change have had a broad approach where staff members have had frequent opportunities to influence the process – thereby developing ownership and motivation for it. Agencies must be aware that little change will occur unless they create an institutional culture favourable to change: *this will only happen if explicit effort is dedicated to fostering and managing change*.

*Possible action points*

■ *Determined leadership at both political and policy-making levels should capture and channel the interest and commitment of all staff, other government bodies and civil society to focus more resolutely and forcefully on supporting poverty reduction in partner countries.*

■ *Develop a clear agency vision, policy framework and strategy for attacking poverty.*

■ *Tensions exist where agencies have multiple objectives (for example sustainable development, poverty reduction, gender equality, conflict, or national foreign policy goals). Top management needs to clarify objectives and consult widely with staff in doing so, as a way of identifying complementarities, addressing trade-offs and resolving differences in the ensuing debates.*

■ *It is essential to link human resources staff with policy staff: leadership must understand the practical implications of strategy and policy in terms of the way staff are managed and human resources renewed.*

■ *There is a need for leaders at all levels of the agency – and particularly at middle management level – to clearly flag their commitment to poverty reduction.*

## Retooling institutional systems and processes

**Institutional systems and processes – such as project screening and approval procedures, staff regulations, and terms of reference for consultants and research – should directly link with agency poverty reduction goals.**

Development organisations have many systems for organising, controlling and facilitating their work and for managing people. Poverty reduction goals should be integrated into these systems to reinforce focus and discipline.

*Possible action points*

■ *The goal of reducing poverty should inform all planning processes (including country strategies, sector approaches and project interventions) within the agency. Programmes and projects should be systematically assessed for their potential to reduce poverty in all agency screening and approval procedures.*

■ *Consider revisions and additions to staff regulations that reinforce the role of reducing poverty as central to agency objectives, operations and performance.*

■ *Promote an institutional culture that supports poverty reduction. A "disbursement" culture or a culture that treats poverty reduction with only lip-service can dilute or undermine the agency's focus on it. Develop approaches, instruments or strategies that accommodate or reduce disbursement pressures at the end of the agency fiscal year.*

■ *Terms of reference for research, studies or programme preparation should make links to poverty reduction goals. Build targets and standards for poverty reduction into contractual arrangements and partnership agreements with external agencies, NGOs and consultants. These agreements should incorporate incentives and sanctions, and have clear systems for monitoring results.*

## New capacities and skill requirements

The *DAC Scoping Study* found that agencies have not necessarily assessed whether the mix and level of their skills are consistent with their poverty reduction priorities and with new ways of working. The skills required will depend on how an agency is organised and on what approaches it is considering as the best ones for effective poverty reduction.

An agency-wide "skills appraisal" will identify skills to be acquired or deepened, either through training, recruitment, consultancy services, exchanges or secondments with other partners. Staff with broader ranges of specialist skills (including knowledge relevant to the cross-cutting concerns of gender, environment and governance, as well as participatory approaches) will be needed. The poverty reduction agenda will put greater emphasis on working through multidisciplinary teams (which requires team-building skills). It will also call for improved staff capacity to interpret quantitative and qualitative information on poverty and apply cross-disciplinary knowledge.

Beyond skill acquisition, deliberate actions are needed to bring skills together. This means strengthening staff capacity to integrate macro and sector-specific information, to combine specialist and generalist knowledge by fostering cross-fertilisation through team work, and to provide specialist expertise at country level at critical junctures in the planning and implementation process.

**Addressing poverty will call for a broader range of specialist skills (such as participatory development, statistical capacity-building and governance) and efforts to bring skills together at country level through multidisciplinary teamwork.**

*Possible action points*

■ *Work with the existing agency skills set, assisting sector staff to acquire and integrate poverty reduction skills in their work.*

■ *Focus on "new skills" building:*

  • *For partnership: skills in facilitation and co-ordination and in relationship-building (such as active listening, consensus-building, negotiation, diplomacy).*

  • *For diplomatic staff: skills for understanding development issues, for taking risks, and for interacting with partners in the field.*

  • *For all operational staff: skills to enhance flexibility, adaptability, self-criticism, and lateral thinking.*

■ *Addressing the many dimensions of poverty calls for building and deploying multidisciplinary teams at country level with competence and skills in many domains. Bring skills together at macro, meso and micro levels.*

■ *Staff recruitment (for permanent, temporary and diplomatic staff) should focus on poverty reduction skills and performance, team-working capacities, and experience in co-ordination (facilitation, listening and negotiating skills).*

■ *Encourage the development of staff "conductors" who can link field skills and knowledge to policy analysis at headquarters – thereby providing a "reality check" for agency policy development.*

**New skills for building partnership "capacity" at the field level include skills in facilitation, co-ordination, diplomacy, active listening, consensus-building and negotiation.**

## Structures

Poverty is multidimensional, calling for actions in a range of areas, such as health, education, infrastructure, micro-enterprise development and empowerment. Comprehensive, holistic strategies that address these dimensions across different sectors, regions and social groups are needed. This is very different from "traditional" aid modalities based on a unidimensional, relatively simple suite of project interventions. The shift means that agencies will need to have greater knowledge of partner countries (including from the perspective of poor people themselves) and a sound understanding of sectoral issues, intersectoral links and good practice.

**An effective organisational structure for dealing with the many dimensions of poverty facilitates the exchange of knowledge, cross-fertilisation of expertise and improved co-ordination.**

Implementing an effective, multidimensional strategy for fighting poverty can be powerfully enhanced by an organisational structure that facilitates the exchange of knowledge, the cross-fertilisation of expertise and improved co-ordination. Present organisational structures that typically divide staff into autonomous, isolated units dealing with sectoral development or geographic zones hinder exchange, synergies and coherence.

Agencies have developed four structural approaches for enhancing their overall institutional capacity to address poverty, in large part drawn from good practice with mainstreaming gender:

- A specialised unit charged with mainstreaming poverty reduction.

- "Champions" or "focal points" to facilitate action and institutional change (often working closely with the specialised unit).

- Combining poverty reduction "champions" and units with agency-wide staff responsibility for promoting poverty reduction.

- Developing a "light" matrix structure combining poverty reduction (a programme structure) with a geographical/regional set-up (a functional structure).

**Multidisciplinary teams for field work, and "knowledge networks" for sharing information and lessons learned throughout the agency, are both potentially powerful organisational tools.**

Other, more flexible structural devices can be used to great advantage in mobilising diverse expertise and knowledge for addressing poverty. Multidisciplinary teams (assembled to accomplish specific tasks) and "knowledge networks" (created to share information and lessons learned throughout the agency) are potentially powerful instruments for enhancing poverty reduction impact. These devices will have further implications for the ways agency staff are deployed and collaborate with one another, and for access to technology and training.

No single structural approach is more effective than any other, since the ways and the context in which they are implemented vary so greatly. At the same time, structure is more than the constituent pieces of a simple organisational chart. It also includes managing the interfaces or the "white space"[6] around the boxes in the organisational chart. Agencies are bound to end up with a variety of structures, each responding to individual agency constraints and organisational needs.

*Possible action points*

- *Encourage team-working across professional boundaries to address more effectively the multidimensional nature of poverty and to overcome narrow single-sector-driven or supply-led approaches.*

**Organisational structures (such as poverty reduction "focal points", networks or units) are very important, but informal working methods – which determine how people work together in groups and across the organisation – matter most.**

- *Develop structures and mechanisms for mainstreaming poverty reduction. Poverty reduction "champions" can be used to raise the profile of poverty reduction within the agency, to provide advice, to strengthen communication between and across organisational levels, and to promote good practice. Resources and authority must be vested in agency poverty reduction advocates.*

- *Flatter, simpler organisational structures are more compatible with trends towards team work, developing and valuing multidisciplinary competence in staff and greater reliance on information flows and networking. At the same time, some hierarchy is needed to ensure accountability, quality control and leadership.*

- *It is essential to understand that while organisational structures are very important, informal working methods – which determine how people work together in groups and across organisational structures – matter most.*

## Aligning Human Resource Management practices with the poverty reduction goal

HRM plays a key role in channelling, strengthening and renewing the most valuable asset an organisation has: its staff. Performance management, reward and incentive systems and training have far-reaching impacts on staff motivation and capacity. They are central aspects of human resource management policies that should be aligned with agency poverty reduction objectives.

### Performance management and incentives

Staff performance management, monitoring, evaluation and rewards are support processes and systems found in all organisations. Work gets done through both management practices and these primary support processes. When an organisation's processes and systems for performance are not defined, designed and managed, there is no context for – or driver of – human and system performance. In such an environment, well-intentioned activities are carried out in a vacuum. They are frequently off the mark.

Often organisational goals and strategies are not linked with processes such as performance management or reward systems. The *DAC Scoping Study* found that agencies did not link incentives and rewards to the goal of poverty reduction. As a result, the drive for poverty reduction tends to vary considerably from department to department, from country programme to country programme, and from person to person. In these circumstances, there is little fit between the organisation's commitment to poverty reduction goals and its monitoring and evaluation processes or its reward systems.

Taking serious account in staff assessments of the performance of individual staff members in reducing poverty, working as effective partners and promoting policy coherence will call for careful consideration of relevant criteria and benchmarks. Periodic management monitoring of staff and agency evaluation systems can play a key role in providing information on which assessments can be based. Performance linked to poverty reduction should, as much as possible, focus on *impact*. This creates challenges, since attribution of causal effects to a specific agency's actions may be difficult to determine empirically. Evaluation methodologies assessing progress and achievements in supporting country efforts to reduce poverty will need to be developed, including indications of proximate measures when causality cannot be established.

It is a challenge to translate agency objectives (such as poverty reduction) or institutional values (such as team-building, partnership skills, etc.) into staff performance indicators. This can be facilitated if objectives and related performance criteria at different hierarchical levels (such as directorates, sections, divisions, units, etc.) are directly linked to overarching institutional objectives and values. Such a "cascading" performance management system will tighten and amplify institution-wide efforts to deliver on poverty reduction goals and foster partnership attitudes and reflexes.

Rewards and incentives are important in moulding and reinforcing staff behaviour and play a key role in driving performance. Non-monetary rewards could include greater choice as regards job assignments or postings abroad, more challenging and more interesting jobs, greater visibility, increased time to pursue related professional interests, access to special training for expanding career options, sponsoring research or advanced studies, promotion, etc.

**Staff performance management, agency reward and incentive systems, and training efforts – which have far-reaching impact on staff motivation and capacity – should be aligned with agency poverty reduction and partnership objectives.**

*Possible action points*

■ *Strengthen the links between the agency's strategic objectives, its unit business plans, and individual staff performance "results agreements" to increase internal coherence and consolidate efforts.*

■ *Country directors and programme managers should have clear poverty reduction and partnership goals in their briefs, in their performance assessments and in their criteria for assessing the performance of their staff.*

■ *Credible performance management systems are based on objective criteria. Where poverty reduction performance is a criterion, agency evaluation systems may need to focus on developing methodologies for assessing poverty reduction impact.*

■ *Incentive systems should be flexible and of a facilitative/regulatory nature.*

■ *It is important to identify and understand institutional incentives and counter-incentives (both explicit and implicit) when evaluating measures to increase coherence between agency poverty reduction objectives and staff performance.*

### Learning and training

**Moving a bureaucracy to a new mode of operating calls for sensitising all staff to poverty issues, helping them "identify" with new organisational values and goals, and strengthening the agency's skill base.**

In order to move a bureaucracy to a new mode of operating, there must be a great deal of learning and training about the new operating and institutional environment. Staff will need to become sensitised to poverty issues and concerns. They will need to learn how to "identify" themselves with new organisational goals, values and commitments. Individuals will need to develop new skills. Training can also play an important role in improving aid effectiveness through the transmission of good practices and lessons learned.

Poverty reduction training should be tailored to suit the needs of different audiences:

■ Introductory courses for general staff, newcomers and field staff (including those employed locally) provide basic training in poverty: its dimensions, its magnitude, basic approaches for tackling it, etc. These courses are important for building an understanding of the agency's institutional mission and values regarding the poverty reduction objective.

■ Refresher courses for junior staff with limited experience, for staff wishing to broaden their development knowledge and for field staff (including local hires) can bring them up to speed with such issues as the Millennium Development Goals, new poverty concepts and approaches, the shift from projects to programming approaches, how to design and implement support, and so on. This training deepens operational staff competence so they can work more effectively as part of a team.

■ Technical specialists require targeted, more in-depth training to deepen their knowledge and skills and to help them come abreast with contemporary research and experience.

■ Training for consultants, for professionals from other parts of government and for civil society is also necessary to sensitise them to poverty concepts, needs and challenges and, in particular, to help them understand how reducing poverty intersects with their work.

*Possible action points*

- *Training programmes should promote poverty reduction awareness-raising of all staff and enhance operational skills for specialist staff.*

- *Agencies can share training and learning events with one another and with partners. Collaboration on specific training courses is especially useful at the country level, and can be linked to local poverty reduction strategy development exercises. Planning and training should go hand-in-hand.*

- *Agencies should exchange information about their training tools, approaches and products, making them available in the public domain (such as a website) where others can "pick and choose", adapting materials to their specific institutional needs.*

- *Training courses for poverty reduction trainers are very important, and could be developed and implemented in collaboration with a number of agencies.*

- *"Hands-on" training methods and action learning programmes that focus on solving actual problems at the field level have proved highly effective.*

- *Allocate staff time to learn about and share good practice in development, and facilitate their access to knowledge, research and evaluation results.*

**Sharing training and leaning events with other agencies and partners and exchanging information about training tools, approaches and products can improve the quality and cost-effectiveness of training efforts.**

## The way ahead: working as partners

Partnership is leading a number of DAC Members to shift the centre of gravity for policy development and decision-making to the field. It is also highlighting the need to reduce burdens that agency institutional procedures and controls create for partner governments. These have direct implications for changes in agency institutional systems, structures and capacities.

### Decentralisation

The move to partnership and promoting country ownership is prompting agencies to decentralise decision-making and staff to the field. Decentralisation helps agencies to improve their understanding of, and to heighten their responsiveness to, changing local poverty conditions. It also promotes better dialogue and partnership through close and continuous interaction with other local partners and it strengthens agency credibility as a partner. Experience has shown that while decentralisation has high costs, *it has high returns*.

Decentralisation affects a number of processes, such as decision-making and communications. It means granting greater budgetary flexibility and decentralising authority and capacity to negotiate with local partners. Staff deployment, information flow and accountability frameworks are all issues commonly mentioned by agencies that have gone through, or are going through, this process.

Decentralisation creates new tasks and responsibilities for country managers and their staff, new roles for headquarters and new ways of working between headquarters and the field. These new work demands require rethinking the way work is currently organised, including formal and informal organisational arrangements.

**Decentralising decision-making and staff to the field is an important impetus to fostering strong partnership relationships and promoting local ownership of policy choices and implementation.**

## Box 19. Tips for making decentralisation work

Key elements for successful decentralisation include:

■ A clear policy framework and a strong "centre" with decisive ideas about how to decentralise control and operations.

■ Good "people and process" managers at headquarters and in the field.

■ Flexibility to transform staff roles and tasks at headquarters.

■ Field office staff with the right skills mix (including a broad understanding of development issues, personal effectiveness skills, specialist expertise, and good knowledge of the local partner country context and of the current workings of their agency at headquarters level).

■ Good telecommunications (intranet, efficient management information systems, teleconferencing, thematic virtual networks).

■ Regular face-to-face meetings among country, regional and headquarters staff.

■ Field staff should have "counterpart" staff in headquarters to facilitate exchange of information and access to headquarters' services, and to strengthen institutional identity and solidarity.

■ Embassy staff should be trained and empowered to make informed decisions, manage change processes and create countervailing power.

---

■ Field staff – including diplomatic personnel – need adequate expertise and knowledge to make informed decisions on programming and to interact effectively with local counterparts. This has implications for recruitment, training, the deployment of experts or teams and for the capacity of field offices to manage financial transactions.

■ Headquarters will need to shift towards "letting go" of transactions and relationships and focusing instead on overall strategic management, "servicing" field staff with adequate and timely information and resources, setting policies and standards, having a light system of quality assurance, facilitating access to communications and networks, managing procurement systems and taking the lead on promoting policy coherence across their government ministries and departments. Country desks will need to be strengthened to enable staff to manage the large variety of new tasks decentralisation creates.

**In a decentralised agency, headquarters tasks shift from managing transactions and relationships to focusing on overall strategic management, facilitating access to communications and networks and promoting government-wide policy coherence.**

Decentralisation means redoubling efforts to co-ordinate local dialogue and negotiations to ensure meetings will not proliferate – and unduly tax government capacity. It will call for prudent management of locally hired field staff – to prevent work overload, to refrain from depleting the local skill base and to offer career development opportunities. It will call for creative efforts to help headquarters' organisational culture and vision become embedded in the mind-set of *all* field office staff. And it will heighten the need to improve mechanisms for continuous learning at different levels in the agency, for the dissemination of knowledge, and for *ensuring lessons learned are implemented throughout a decentralised management structure.* Box 19 highlights good practice for decentralising decision-making and management to the field.

Decentralisation decisions will have to weigh implicit benefits with potential downside factors, such as increased costs and overstretched institutional technical expertise. It is also not necessarily a feasible or an appropriate solution for smaller agencies. This argues all the more strongly for increasing collaboration and sharing expertise and information among all agencies, and for relying more on local expertise.

*Possible action points*

■ *The process and pace of decentralisation will depend on agency leadership impetus, organisational set-ups, institutional culture and history, and the context in the partner country.*

■ *Information needs are heightened when agencies decentralise (networking and communications are more important, two-way information flows become essential, staff must maintain links and raise awareness of these links at headquarters).*

■ *It is important to address up-front HRM challenges implicit in decentralisation (such as selection criteria for field staff, appropriate financial incentives for field postings, career development for local staff, re-entry from the field, etc.).*

■ *Globalisation has impelled many private corporations to decentralise their operations: evaluations and case studies of their experience could be helpful to agency efforts to decentralise.*

## Reducing the burdens agencies create for their partners

Multiple administrative requirements and poor agency co-ordination of policies and activities create heavy burdens for partner governments, particularly in those countries where numerous agencies are active. The emerging consensus on country ownership of strategies for reducing poverty increases the need to simplify and harmonise practices, procedures and reporting requirements in line with agency accountability requirements.

There is often a concomitant need to support partner country capacity-building efforts (for example in financial management, accounting, monitoring, etc.) to ensure transparency and accountability to stakeholders. This capacity-building should reach beyond the public sector to the private sector and civil society (such as professional associations) as well. Stronger local administrative capacity and probity will strengthen agency confidence to align their systems and procedures with those of their developing country partners. Members should give consideration, in collaboration with other Members, to reforming their administrative requirements and increasing their financial flexibility. Such changes are essential to respond to the challenges of *country ownership* of poverty reduction strategies and *partnership arrangements*.

> **Simplifying and harmonising aid management procedures and requirements in line with agency accountability requirements is a *sine qua non* for partnership.**

*Possible action points*

■ *Agencies should help to build partner country capacity to manage and be accountable for development assistance, including reporting and auditing. As capacity improves and agency confidence in local accountability and transparency strengthens, progressive movement towards more flexible agency control mechanisms (such as accepting partners' accounts and/or reporting standards) could be contemplated.*

■ *The scope for closer collaboration among agencies for co-ordinating missions, monitoring and evaluation in a given country should be explored.*

■ *Agencies may need to help partners strengthen their capacity to lead co-ordination.*

# The way ahead: improving institutional capacity to promote policy coherence

**Making sure that other government policies – in such areas a trade, agriculture, environment, migration, debt relief – will not undermine efforts to reduce poverty is a key priority for agencies.**

Success in reducing poverty requires improved policy coherence across OECD Member government policies – not just through development co-operation. Mutually reinforcing policy actions across government departments will create synergies for achieving the international poverty reduction goal. Only this will ensure that Members' efforts to reduce poverty are not undermined by the policies and actions of other parts of their governments.

*Policy coherence* calls for understanding the impacts that different policies have on reducing poverty and for mechanisms to resolve contradictions or to mitigate the effects of conflicting policies. To achieve policy coherence, agencies must improve their mechanisms for co-ordinating with other institutions responsible for issues that have a bearing on reducing poverty (for example trade, agriculture, environment, debt relief, migration). These institutions may be other ministries in the Member country, other agencies in partner countries, or global governance institutions.

Part 4 outlined the importance and procedural steps for increasing policy coherence in DAC Member governments. Bilateral agencies have a key catalytic role in the initiation and implementation of policy coherence across their governments. This has implications for institutional capacity in four focus areas:

- Agencies need to develop internal capacity to identify the role of a given government policy, analyse its impact on poverty, and trace where, within government, the policy can be adjusted for enhanced coherence. Staff time and resources will be needed to carry out this work and to make reasoned judgements about what realistically can be changed. The agency role is one of catalyst and advocate, recognising that countries have a variety of legitimate objectives and that decisions on sensitive issues depend on catalysing support within the relevant ministries and government-wide.

**Promoting policy coherence calls for strengthening agency capacity to elevate policy coherence on the domestic agenda and to deal with inconsistencies and contradictions across government policies.**

- Mechanisms should be developed to permit closer communications and consultations with a wide range of government ministries, departments and agencies in order to resolve policy contradictions and inconsistencies. Good practice calls for creating an authoritative central policy co-ordinating unit to establish strong linkages among government bodies for this purpose.

- Agency capacity to influence others should be strengthened as much as possible in order to elevate policy coherence on the domestic policy agenda and to deal with government policy contradictions and inconsistencies. This will call for skills in addressing complex policy coherence issues, evaluating trade-offs and negotiating consensual decisions among different OECD government departments and ministries that recognise development concerns.

- Greater attention is needed to improve coherence within the aid system itself, ensuring that the policies and decisions undertaken by other ministries with responsibilities for aspects of development assistance, by implementing agencies, and by Member country representatives in the governing bodies of multilateral development institutions are consistent and compatible with the poverty reduction objective.

*Possible action points*

■ *Leadership must seek support at the highest governmental levels in order to ensure that other government ministries and departments consider development perspectives in formulating their policies. They should also seek this support for strengthening mechanisms for co-ordinating policy with other governmental bodies, resolving conflicts and developing ways and means for dealing with policy contradictions or conflicts.*

■ *Staff capacity for understanding the implications of different government policies should be deepened.*

■ *Agency staff should be sensitised to the importance of policy coherence issues and encouraged to promote greater coherence in their sphere of action and influence.*

## Conclusion

Mainstreaming poverty reduction, partnership and policy coherence throughout agency policies and operations calls for aligning institutional structures, systems and management practices behind these objectives. But institutional change should not stop at the boundaries of the agency. It needs to affect as well interactions *among* bilateral agencies, since aid effectiveness and partnership are contingent on co-operating and collaborating more actively with one another. This means understanding much more about how each agency works – in order to discover similarities and overlap in the way business is conducted. This, in turn, will enable agencies to explore the scope for strengthening synergies and complementarities, for leveraging each other's strengths, and for sharing "the work".

**Institutional change should not stop at the boundaries of the agency: it needs to affect interactions between bilateral agencies so as to deepen partnerships among agencies, to improve aid synergies and to leverage each other's strengths.**

# Notes

1.  "Mainstreaming" poverty reduction means integrating it as a critical consideration in agency policy formulation, planning, decision-making, implementation, and evaluation processes.

2.  The contents of Part 5 are based on the outcome of a special POVNET workshop held in February 2001 dealing with institutional change issues that was attended by agency upper management, operational and human resource management staff.

3.  This agenda, described in Parts 1 to 4 of the *Guidelines*, calls for working in partnership with other development actors to support country-owned and -led strategies for reducing poverty.

4.  HRM systems are a key part of formal organisational arrangements and include compensation, benefits, incentives, performance management, job design, recruitment, career development and training.

5.  The 25 case studies that form the basis of the *DAC Scoping Study of Donor Poverty Reduction Policies and Practices* (1999) provide numerous examples of how agencies are making changes in their organisations.

6.  The boxes in an organisational chart show *i)* how people are grouped together for operational efficiency and *ii)* reporting relationships, which typically suggest a hierarchy of responsibilities and functions. The "white space" refers to interfaces above, below and to either side of these boxes that cut across functional boundaries – and through which the actual work of an organisation gets done, such as when policy from one department at headquarters is passed to a group in the field to implement. "White space" also refers to management practices and human resource management systems that guide and motivate staff performance – and that in another dimension, cut across functional boundaries and have a formative impact on the way in which work gets done.

## Appendix: Millennium Development Goals (MDGs

| GOALS AND TARGETS | INDICATORS |
|---|---|
| **GOAL 1: ERADICATE EXTREME POVERTY AND HUNGER** | |
| **Target 1.** Halve, between 1990 and 2015, the proportion of people whose income is less than $1 a day | 1. Proportion of population below one dollar per day<br>2. Poverty gap ratio [incidence x depth of poverty]<br>3. Share of poorest quintile in national consumption |
| **2.** Halve, between 1990 and 2015, the proportion of people who suffer from hunger | 4. Prevalence of underweight children (under five years of age)<br>5. Proportion of population below minimum level of dietary energy consumption |
| **GOAL 2: ACHIEVE UNIVERSAL PRIMARY EDUCATION** | |
| **Target 3.**. Ensure that, by 2015, children everywhere, boys and girls alike, will be able to complete a full course of primary schooling | 6. Net enrolment ratio in primary education<br>7. Proportion of pupils starting grade 1 who reach grade 5<br>8. Literacy rate of 15-24 year-olds |
| **GOAL 3: PROMOTE GENDER EQUALITY AND EMPOWER WOMEN** | |
| **Target 4.** Eliminate gender disparity in primary and secondary education preferably by 2005 and to all levels of education no later than 2015 | 9. Ratio of girls to boys in primary, secondary and tertiary education<br>10. Ratio of literate females to 15-24 year-old males<br>11. Share of women in wage employment in the non-agricultural sector<br>12. Proportion of seats held by women in national parliament |
| **GOAL 4: REDUCE CHILD MORTALITY** | |
| **Target 5.** Reduce by two-thirds, between 1990 and 2015, the under-five mortality rate | 13. Under-five mortality rate<br>14. Infant mortality rate<br>15. Proportion of 1-year-old children immunised against measles |
| **GOAL 5: IMPROVE MATERNAL HEALTH** | |
| **Target 6.** Reduce by three-quarters, between 1990 and 2015, the maternal mortality ratio | 16. Maternal mortality ratio<br>17. Proportion of births attended by skilled health personnel |
| **GOAL 6: COMBAT HIV/AIDS, MALARIA AND OTHER DISEASES** | |
| **Target 7.** Have halted by 2015, and begun to reverse, the spread of HIV/AIDS | 18. HIV prevalence among 15-24 year-old pregnant women<br>19. Contraceptive prevalence rate<br>20. Number of children orphaned by HIV/AIDS |
| **8.** Have halted by 2015, and begun to reverse, the incidence of malaria and other major diseases | 21. Prevalence and death rates associated with malaria<br>22. Proportion of population in malaria risk areas using effective malaria prevention and treatment measures<br>23. Prevalence and death rates associated with tuberculosis<br>24. Proportion of TB cases detected and cured under DOTS (Directly Observed Treatment Short Course) |

## Appendix: Millennium Development Goals (MDGs) (continued)

| GOALS AND TARGETS | INDICATORS |
|---|---|

### GOAL 7: ENSURE ENVIRONMENTAL SUSTAINABILITY*

**Target 9.** Integrate the principles of sustainable development into country policies and programmes and reverse the loss of environmental resources

25. Proportion of land area covered by forest

26. Land area protected to maintain biological diversity

27. GDP per unit of energy use (as proxy for energy efficiency)

28. Carbon dioxide emissions (per capita) [Plus two figures of global atmospheric pollution: ozone depletion and the accumulation of global warming gases]

29. Proportion of population with sustainable access to an improved water source

**10.** Halve, by 2015, the proportion of people without sustainable access to safe drinking water

30. Proportion of people with access to improved sanitation

**11.** By 2020, have achieved a significant improvement in the lives of at least 100 million slum-dwellers

31. Proportion of people with access to secure tenure [Urban/rural disaggregation of several of the above indicators may be relevant for monitoring improvement in the lives of slum-dwellers]

### GOAL 8: DEVELOP A GLOBAL PARTNERSHIP FOR DEVELOPMENT*

**Target 12.** Develop further an open, rule-based, predictable, non-discriminatory trading and financial system Includes a commitment to good governance, development, and poverty reduction – both nationally and internationally

*Some of the indicators listed below will be monitored separately for the Least Developed Countries (LDCs), Africa, landlocked countries and small island developing states.*

**Official Development Assistance**

32. Net ODA as percentage of DAC donors' GNI [targets of 0.7% in total and 0.15% for LDCs]

33. Proportion of ODA to basic social services (basic education, primary health care, nutrition, safe water and sanitation)

**13.** Address the special needs of the least developed countries
Includes: tariff and quota free access for LDC exports; enhanced programme of debt relief for HIPC and cancellation of official bilateral debt; and more generous ODA for countries committed to poverty reduction

34. Proportion of ODA that is untied

35. Proportion of ODA for environment in small island developing states

36. Proportion of ODA for transport sector in landlocked countries

**Market access**

37. Proportion of exports (by value and excluding arms) admitted free of duties and quotas

**14.** Address the special needs of landlocked countries and small island developing states
(through Barbados Programme and 22nd General Assembly provisions)

38. Average tariffs and quotas on agricultural products and textiles and clothing

39. Domestic and export agricultural subsidies in OECD countries

40. Proportion of ODA provided to help build trade capacity

## Appendix: Millennium Development Goals (MDGs) (continued)

| GOALS AND TARGETS | INDICATORS |
|---|---|
| **GOAL 8: (continued)** | **Debt sustainability** |
| **Target 15.** Deal comprehensively with the debt problems of developing countries through national and international measures in order to make debt sustainable in the long term | 41. Proportion of official bilateral HIPC debt cancelled<br>42. Debt service as a percentage of exports of goods and services<br>43. Proportion of ODA provided as debt relief<br>44. Number of countries reaching HIPC decision and completion points |
| **16.** In co-operation with developing countries, develop and implement strategies for decent and productive work for youth | 45. Unemployment rate of 15-24 year-olds |
| **17.** In co-operation with pharmaceutical companies, provide access to affordable, essential drugs in developing countries | 46. Proportion of population with access to affordable essential drugs on a sustainable basis |
| **18.** In co-operation with the private sector, make available the benefits of new technologies, especially information and communications | 47. Telephone lines per 1 000 people<br>48. Personal computers per 1 000 people<br>Other Indicators TBD |

*\* The selection of indicators for Goals 7 and 8 is subject to further refinement.*

# DAC Guidelines

The OECD Development Assistance Committee adopts policy guidance for Members in the conduct of their development co-operation programmes. These guidelines reflect the views and experience of the Members and benefit from input by multilateral institutions and individual experts, including experts from developing countries.

## Shaping the 21st Century: The Contribution of Development Co-operation

Approved by the DAC High Level Meeting of 1996, *Shaping the 21st Century* sets forth strategic orientations for development co-operation into the 21st century. The report recalls the importance of development for people everywhere and the impressive record of human progress during the past 50 years. It suggests a set of basic goals based on UN Conference outcomes – for economic well-being, social development and environmental sustainability – as a vision for the future, and proposes strategies for attaining that vision through partnership in support of self-help efforts, improved co-ordination and consistent policies. These goals, and the partnership approach, have since been widely adopted in the international development system.

In this context, DAC Members have developed a series of guidelines for attaining the ambitious goals set out in *Shaping the 21st Century*.

### The DAC Guidelines (2001):
- *Poverty Reduction*
- *Strategies for Sustainable Development: Guidance for Development Co-operation*
- *Strengthening Trade Capacity for Development*
- *Helping Prevent Violent Conflict*

## Previously Published DAC Guidelines
- *DAC Guidelines for Gender Equality and Women's Empowerment in Development Co-operation*
- *Support of Private Sector Development*
- *Participatory Development and Good Governance*
- *Donor Assistance to Capacity Development in Environment*
- *Guidelines on Aid and Environment:*
   - No. 1: Good Practices for Environmental Impact Assessment of Development Projects
   - No. 2: Good Practices for Country Environmental Surveys and Strategies
   - No. 3: Guidelines for Aid Agencies on Involuntary Displacement and Resettlement in Developing Countries
   - No. 4: Guidelines for Aid Agencies on Global Environmental Problems
   - No. 5: Guidelines for Aid Agencies on Chemicals Management
   - No. 6: Guidelines for Aid Agencies on Pest and Pesticide Management
   - No. 7: Guidelines for Aid Agencies on Disaster Mitigation
   - No. 8: Guidelines for Aid Agencies on Global and Regional Aspects of the Development and Protection of the Marine and Coastal Environment
   - No. 9: Guidelines for Aid Agencies for Improved Conservation and Sustainable Use of Tropical and Sub-Tropical Wetlands

OECD PUBLICATIONS, 2, rue André-Pascal, 75775 PARIS CEDEX 16
PRINTED IN FRANCE
(43 2001 09 1 P) ISBN 92-64-19506-8 – No. 52105 2001